What People Are Saying About
Chicken Soup for the Military Wife's Soul ...

"This book clearly illustrates the pride and sacrifice of the spouses and their families who support our military personnel. *Chicken Soup for the Military Wife's Soul* is a touching celebration of military wives everywhere."

Edgar Mitchell, Capt., USN (Ret.)
Apollo 14 astronaut

"Every woman, military or civilian, will relate to this inspiring collection of true stories. In their own words, the sisterhood of military wives open their hearts and offer a generous helping of their strength, dedication and pride for you to enjoy."

Amy J. Fetzer
author, *Tell It to the Marines*

"For generations, military spouses have been the soldiers without recognition, without a chest full of medals and without rank. This book gives a heartfelt salute to those women steadfastly supporting their active-duty military members. Thank you, *Chicken Soup*, for creating a book for the hundreds of thousands of military spouses worldwide! A true blessing for all of us . . ."

Babette Maxwell
cofounder, *Military Spouses* magazine

"The memories in *Chicken Soup for the Military Wife's Soul* are ones that we may have lived and with which we have great empathy. After reading the book, I needed time to recover from all my tears and memories. Thank you for creating this book of inspiring stories and memories for us to read."

Martha Didamo
national president, Gold Star Wives of America, Inc.

"*Chicken Soup* has created a wonderful, heartfelt collection of stories by military wives to celebrate the contributions and sacrifices that the spouses make while supporting those who defend our country. *Chicken Soup for the Military Wife's Soul* is a powerful tool that will be treasured for years to come. I wholeheartedly recommend this book!"

Rev. Robert A. Schuller
Crystal Cathedral Ministries

CHICKEN SOUP
FOR THE
MILITARY WIFE'S
SOUL

101 Stories to Touch the Heart and Rekindle the Spirit

Jack Canfield
Mark Victor Hansen
Cindy Pedersen
Charles Preston

Health Communications, Inc.
Deerfield Beach, Florida

www.hcibooks.com
www.chickensoup.com

We would like to acknowledge the following publishers and individuals for permission to reprint the following material. (Note: The stories that are in the public domain, or that were written by Jack Canfield, Mark Victor Hansen, Cindy Pedersen or Charles Preston are not included in this listing.)

(Continued on page 323)

The Commissary Roadblock. Reprinted by permission of Catherine Paige Anderson Swiney. ©2003 Catherine Paige Anderson Swiney.

God Bless America . . . and Remember Italy, Too! Reprinted by permission of Stacy Smith Kirchheiner. ©2003 Stacy Smith Kirchheiner.

A Quiet Road and *Somebody Knew Gene.* Reprinted by permission of Sara Rosett. ©2003 Sara Rosett.

The Call Home. Reprinted by permission of Carrie Elizabeth Boggs. ©2003 Carrie Elizabeth Boggs.

Library of Congress Cataloging-in-Publication Data

Chicken soup for the military wife's soul : stories to touch the heart and rekindle
    the spirit / [compiled by] Jack Canfield ... [et al.]
        p. cm.
    ISBN 0-7573-0265-3 (tp.)
        1. Women and the military—United States.   2. Military spouses—United
    States—Biography.   3. Military spouses—United States—Conduct of life.
    4. Inspiration—Anecdotes.   I. Canfield, Jack, 1944-

U21.75.C46 2005
355'.0092'273—dc22
[B]

2005042004

Publisher: Health Communications, Inc.
              3201 S.W. 15th Street
              Deerfield Beach, FL 33442–8190

R-06-05

Cover design by Larissa Hise Henoch
Inside formatting by Lawna Patterson Oldfield

This book is dedicated to
the memory of our most beloved
military wives, our mothers:
Ethel M. Preston and Sophia Shell.

With joy and gratitude,
we also dedicate this book to
military spouses worldwide for their
unconditional love and service.

Contents

Acknowledgments...xiii
Introduction..xvii
Share with Us xxi

1. RED, WHITE AND BLUE

The Commissary Roadblock *Paige Anderson Swiney*......................................2
God Bless America . . . and Remember Italy, Too!
    Stacy Smith Kirchheiner..4
A Quiet Road *Sara Rosett* 7
The Call Home *C. Boggs*...10
Pregnancy *Michele Putman* 12
My Nurse Angel *Lisa Cobb*..14
The Calm During the Storm *Kathy Oberhaus* 17
Miracle Wallet *Lisa Cobb*..19
A Soldier, Someone's Child *Elizabeth Martin, R.N.* 22
All in a Day's Work *Liz Rae* 26

2. I MISS YOU SO

A Navy Wife's Prayer *Sue Groseclose-Combs*..30
Picture the Waiting *Candace Carteen* 31

Letters of Hope *Shelley McEwan* 36

A Chain of Love *Tammy C. Logan* 39

Deployed *Naomi Stanton* 41

Silent Survivors of the Vietnam War *Sally B. Griffis* 44

The Phone Call *Jodie Smith* 47

Hello, Beautiful *Jane Garvey* 50

Free Mail *Jill Cottrell* 52

Mercy *Evangeline Dionisio as told to Shelly Mecum* 55

Navy Pilot's Wife *Sarah Monagle* 58

The Unseen Veteran *Amanda Legg* 61

3. RAISING MILITARY BRATS

The Cost of War in Cheerios *Mary C. Chace* 64

Can't Let Go *Julie Angelo* 67

Strains of Freedom *Tracey L. Sherman* 69

In the Arms of a Soldier *Mary D. Jackson* 73

Hi Daddy *Jessica Blankenbecler* 76

Doubting Thomas *Leah Tucker* 80

My House Is a War Zone *Melissa M. Baumann* 84

Baby's First Words *Sarah Monagle* 88

All in a Day's Duty *Tracey L. Sherman* 90

War Is Not a Game *Michael J. Jett* 93

Daddy's Angels *Tammy Ross* 97

You Are on Speaker Phone *Angela Keane* 99

4. HOLIDAYS—MILITARY STYLE

Red, White and Blue Christmas *Roxanne Chase* 102

Our Matchbox Christmas *Alice Smith* 103

Spouse of a Soldier *Denise J. Hunnell* 108

Angels Shop at Wal-Mart *Jilleen Kesler* 110

A Military Family *Terry Hurley* 112

A Simple Act of Kindness *Jennifer Minor*...............................114

An Extra Chair *Susanna H. Bartee*..116

Christmas—Military-Family Style *Marjorie H. Lewis* 118

The 25 Days of Christmas *Chanda Stelter*................................121

5. HONEY, WE'VE GOT ORDERS

Keep the House *Jennifer Oscar*...124

Honorable Gift *Marilyn Pate* 127

Part of the Navy Means Saying Good-Bye *Sarah Smiley*....................131

Discomboobled Military Mate *Jan Hornung*............................135

The Difference a Year Makes *Megan Armstrong*.......................138

Saying Good-Bye *Kelli Kirwan* 140

The Line Ends Back There *Bill Blankfield, Col., USAF (Ret.)*................143

Our National Anthem *Gail Gross* 146

My Home *Benjamin Pigsley*..148

The Angel Book *Dianne Collier*...150

6. NO LIFE LIKE IT

The Difference *Col. Steven A. Arrington*.....................................154

Wow *Amy Hollingsworth* 157

The Delivery of Finding Strength *Kimberly L. Shaffer* 160

Operation Enduring Freedom *Heidi Boortz*..............................163

Hair Humor *Laura C. Fitch* 166

Footsteps at the Door *Gwen C. Rollings*....................................169

Only Joking *Vicki A. Vadala-Cummings*.....................................172

Thank You *Kristin Spurlock* 175

The Cookie Lady *Linda Valle*..177

The Honeymoon Is Over *Gary Luerding* 179

It'll Be Okay *Tom Phillips*..183

7. UNITED WE STAND

Sacrifices *Amy J. Fetzer*...186

Dreams and Doubts *Sophia Shell, as told to Cindy Shell Pedersen*........189

Bluegrass Parkway *Kim Riley*...193

Terrorist Brownies *Amie Clark*..197

Destination: Military Wife *Bethany Watkins*................................200

Newfound Heroes *Carol Howard*...204

The Angel at the Olive Garden *Diane L. Flowers*.........................207

You Didn't Tell Me *Donna Porter*..209

Hooah *Theresa Doss*..211

8. AN OFFICER AT THE DOOR

His Name Was John *Mary Catherine Carwile*................................216

Anticipation *Judith Hodge Andrews Dennis as told to Marjorie Kramer*....219

Accepting the Folded Flag *Saundra L. Butts*................................223

A Widow's Salvation *Lora Vivas*...226

A Little Thing *Jodi Chappel*...230

Somebody Knew Gene *Sara Rosett*..233

The Christmas Tree *Joanne Danna*..236

A Bittersweet Photograph *Amy Naegeli*......................................239

A Family Like No Other *Ann Hail Norris*.....................................242

War—A Widow's Weeds, a Widow's Words *Patricia Barbee*..............246

I'll Be There with You *Tracy Atkins*..250

9. BEYOND THE CALL OF DUTY

Happiness Was Born a Twin *Mary E. Dess*...................................252

Combat Boots to Keds *Debbie Koharik*.......................................256

Welcome Home! *DeEtta Woffinden Anderson*
    as told to Dahlynn McKowen 261

A Colorful Experience *Nancy Hall*..264
Patriotic Women Bake Cookies *Denise J. Hunnell*....................267
Something to Be Proud Of *Joyce Stark*.....................................270
The Wedding *Krystee Kott* 273
Angel in the Air *Ramiah Johnson* 277
It Took a War *Jan Hornung*...279

10. LIVING YOUR DREAM

Change of Perspective *Sonja R. Ragaller*...................................282
Identity: A Time of Transition *Twink DeWitt*............................284
If I Return *Sharon C. Stephens Trippe* 288
Lollipops *Diane Proulx* 290
Military Family *Shawni Sticca*..293
Mail Call—God's Provision for Intimacy *Martha Pope Gorris*...........297
Grandma's Wisdom *Rachel E. Twenter*......................................301
A Trip to Washington, D.C. *Abigail L. Hammond*.....................303
Standing Tall *Margaret Buchwald* 305

More Chicken Soup? 309
Supporting Others...310
Who Is Jack Canfield?...311
Who Is Mark Victor Hansen? 312
Who Is Cindy Pedersen?...313
Who Is Charles Preston? 314
Contributors...315
Permissions *(continued)* 325

Acknowledgments

The path to *Chicken Soup for the Military Wife's Soul* has been made all the more beautiful by the many "companions" who have been there with us along the way. Our heartfelt gratitude to:

Our families, who have been chicken soup for our souls!

Inga, Travis, Riley, Christopher, Oran and Kyle Canfield for all their love and support.

Patty, Elisabeth and Melanie Hansen, for once again sharing and lovingly supporting us in creating yet another book.

Tina Pedersen-Flores and Anthony Pedersen, for their enthusiasm and support.

Robin, Michelle, Nicole, Julie, Samantha and Morgan Preston for their never-ending encouragement. Kelle Apone-Cohen for her support and input. BMCS Mark Preston for his military advice.

Our publisher, Peter Vegso, for his vision and commitment to bringing *Chicken Soup for the Soul* to the world. Patty Aubery and Russ Kalmaski, for being there on every step of the journey, with love, laughter and endless creativity.

Barbara Lomonaco, for nourishing us with truly wonderful stories and cartoons.

D'ette Corona, for being there to answer any questions along the way.

Patty Hansen, for her thorough and competent handling of the legal and licensing aspects of the *Chicken Soup for the Soul* books. You are magnificent at the challenge!

Laurie Hartman, for being a precious guardian of the *Chicken Soup* brand.

Lisa Drucker, for taking the time to edit the final manuscript. Once again, thank you for all your hard work.

Veronica Romero, Teresa Esparza, Robin Yerian, Jody Emme, Debbie Lefever, Michelle Adams, Dee Dee Romanello, Shanna Vieyra, Lisa Williams, Gina Romanello, Brittany Shaw, Dena Jacobson, Tanya Jones, and Mary McKay, who support Jack's and Mark's businesses with skill and love.

Bret Witter, Elisabeth Rinaldi, Allison Janse, Kathy Grant and Sandra Bark, our editors, for their devotion to excellence.

Terry Burke, Lori Golden, Kelly Johnson Maragni, Tom Galvin, Sean Geary, Randee Feldman, Patricia McConnell, Kim Weiss, Paola Fernandez-Rana, the sales, marketing and PR departments at Health Communications, Inc., for doing such an incredible job supporting our books.

Tom Sand, Claude Choquette and Luc Jutras, who manage year after year to get our books translated into thirty-six languages around the world.

The art department at Health Communications, Inc., for their talent, creativity and unrelenting patience in producing book covers and inside designs that capture the essence of *Chicken Soup*: Larissa Hise Henoch, Lawna Patterson Oldfield, Andrea Perrine Brower, Anthony Clausi and Dawn Von Strolley Grove.

Tori Newby-Gonzalez for her knowledge and creativity in producing our Web site: *www.militarysoul.org*.

All the *Chicken Soup for the Soul* coauthors, who make it so much of a joy to be part of this *Chicken Soup* family.

Our dedicated volunteer panel of readers who assisted us in making the final selections with invaluable suggestions on how to improve the book: We greatly appreciate the countless hours spent to help us select the very, very best stories. Precia Pedersen, Tom Hamner, Pam Towne, Ivy Ericksen, Teresa Tharp, Jim Rigwald, Kathy Kortus, Lois Draeger, Colette Prokop, Shannon Kortus, Susie Monaster, Mary and Larry Harmon, Louis Brandt, Jennifer Kaiser, Joanne and Samantha Struthers, Pamela Riser and Sister Mary Kamperschroer, who read hundreds of the initial stories that were submitted. To Suzanne Shell, David Beardsley, Peggy Glance, Marsha Blessing, Julia Downie, Teresa Garibay, Robert Flores, Kristy Morehead, Diane Goodwin, Becky Matter, Bonnie Schmitz, Lois Martin, Karla Kay, Shelly Nelson, Cynthia Burnette, Jodi McHugh, Kathleen Kurgan, Cindy Saunders, EOCS Michelle Rhodes, Francis Harvey, Karen and Walt Waltman, LaRayne Lockwood, Tammy Shea, Sharon Spever, Jennifer Castillo, Lisa Wirsching, Katie Korka, Edie Cuttler, Tammy Logan, Sonny Goodwin, Joan Clayton, Sharon Castiglione, Christine Dahl, Becky L. Alexander-Conrad, Teri Detwiler, Christine Crowley and Gloria Dahl, for reading and ranking the final stories.

And, most of all, everyone who submitted their heartfelt stories, poems, quotes and cartoons for possible inclusion in this book. While we were not able to use everything you sent in, we know that each word came from a magical place flourishing within your soul. May the spirit of nature carry you gently toward peace!

Because of the size of this project, we may have left out the names of some people who contributed along the way. If so, we are sorry, but please know that we really do appreciate you very much.

We are truly grateful and love you all!

Introduction

Virtually every individual has been touched at some time by a relative, friend or coworker serving in the armed forces. Everyone has heard the stories and seen the TV or newspaper coverage of tearful farewells as troops leave for battle, of children missing the daily routine with a parent, or of the lonely spouse keeping the home fire burning. There are currently more than 18 million spouses of the 30 million Americans who have served in the U.S. Armed Forces. These are the "silent ranks" that *also* serve as they remain at home nurturing the family.

Thanks to the high-tech mechanization of military equipment and state-of-the-art military intelligence, how we defend our freedom and fight our wars has changed dramatically in the last century. Instead of marching into battle to engage in hand-to-hand combat, we now utilize unmanned aircraft for surveillance, computer-controlled rockets, heat-sensing missiles and night-vision goggles. Reporters are embedded with the troops, bringing the reality of combat into our living rooms daily with graphic, live coverage from the war zone. These compelling images alternate between reassuring us and generating additional anxiety.

Methods of communication have also taken a quantum

leap forward. Modern devices such as camera cell phones, e-mail, satellite phones, digital cameras and Web cameras enable spouses to remain in frequent contact with each other. Unlike our parents and grandparents who waited several months for a letter to cross the ocean, today's troops have almost instant access to their families and loved ones. They have the ability to view the birth of their child from the delivery room via the Internet, or partici-pate in a party by singing "Happy Birthday" via satellite phone.

What remains unchanged is the vast spectrum of human emotions felt by the troops and their families—the faith and fear, the love and loneliness, the pride and per-severance, the courage and camaraderie, the indepen-dence and uncertainty that are a part of everyday life.

The idea of producing *Chicken Soup for the Military Wife's Soul* was conceived shortly after the horrific events of 9/11. We wanted to recognize and inspire the spouses of the troops who defend our freedom.

We reached out to the military community and were overwhelmed by the response. Thousands of heartfelt stories poured into our mailbox—stories about overcom-ing fears, helping other wives adapt to military life and giving back to those less fortunate. As we read each story, we shared the entire spectrum of emotions. We laughed and cried as we experienced their joy and tears, their faith and fear, their courage and strength.

The sisterhood of military wives portrays an ethos that is the hallmark of the spouses who devote their lives to supporting those who defend our country. We honor and deeply respect each of them.

We are grateful to all who shared their deepest feelings in order for us to publish stories that will acknowledge and entertain current military spouses and all who have gone before them. These shared feelings will also provide a legacy of experiences to encourage and support all of those who will follow them.

It is our sincere hope that as you read these stories, each will touch your heart and rekindle your spirit. We invite you to share, with every military spouse you know, this tribute to the pride and honor of those who continuously support our troops.

God bless America.

Share with Us

We would like to invite you to send us stories you would like to see published in future editions of *Chicken Soup for the Soul.*

We would also love to hear your reactions to the stories in this book. Please let us know what your favorite stories are and how they affected you.

Please send submissions to:

Chicken Soup for the Soul
P.O. Box 30880
Santa Barbara, CA 93130
fax: 805-563-2945

You can also visit the *Chicken Soup for the Soul* Web site at:

www.chickensoup.com

We hope you enjoy reading this book as much as we enjoyed compiling, editing and writing it.

1

RED, WHITE AND BLUE

In a world where there is so much to be done, I felt strongly impressed that there must be something for me to do.

Dorothea Dix

The Commissary Roadblock

Time is a dressmaker specializing in alterations.

Faith Baldwin

It was just another harried Wednesday afternoon trip to the commissary. My husband was off teaching young men to fly. My daughters went about their daily activities knowing I would return to them at the appointed time, bearing, among other things, their favorite fruit snacks, frozen pizza and all the little extras that never had to be written down on a grocery list. My grocery list, by the way, was in my sixteen-month-old daughter's mouth, and I was lamenting the fact that the next four aisles of needed items would have to come from memory.

I was turning onto the hygiene/baby aisle while extracting the last of my list out of my daughter's mouth when I nearly ran over an old man. He clearly had no appreciation for the fact that I had forty-five minutes left to finish the grocery shopping, pick up my four-year-old from tumbling class and get to school, where my twelve-year-old and her carpool mates would be waiting.

The man was standing in front of the soap selection,

staring blankly as if he'd never had to choose a bar of soap in his life. I was ready to bark an order at him when I realized there was a tear on his face. Instantly, this grocery-aisle roadblock transformed into a human.

"Can I help you find something?" I asked. He hesitated, and then told me he was looking for soap.

"Any one in particular?" I continued.

"Well, I'm trying to find my wife's brand of soap." I was about to lend him my cell phone so he could call her when he said, "She died a year ago, and I just want to smell her again."

Chills ran down my spine. I don't think the twenty-two-thousand pound mother of all bombs could have had the same impact. As tears welled up in my eyes, my half-eaten grocery list didn't seem so important. Neither did fruit snacks or frozen pizza. I spent the remainder of my time in the commissary that day listening to a man tell the story of how important his wife was to him—and how she took care of their children while he fought for our country.

My life was forever changed that day.

Sometimes the monotony of laundry, housecleaning, grocery shopping and taxi driving leave military wives feeling empty—the kind of emptiness that is rarely fulfilled when our husbands don't want to or can't talk about work. We need to be reminded, at times, of the important role we fill for our family and for our country. Every time my husband comes home too late or leaves before the crack of dawn, I try to remember the sense of importance I felt in the commissary.

Even a retired, decorated World War II pilot who served in missions to protect Americans needed the protection of the woman who served him at home.

Paige Anderson Swiney

God Bless America . . . and Remember Italy, Too!

Culture is both an intellectual phenomenon and a moral one.

Raisa Gorbachev

My husband is in the navy, and, in January 2003, we were transferred to Gaeta, Italy. The culture shock was unbelievable. It took a long time to get used to things, and soon after my husband moved us here, he was shipped out. My four children and I were alone in this strange world. I had to get used to the people, the driving and the food. While I was out having a meal, asking myself if it was all worth it, an old man walked up and asked if he could join me. I agreed, smiling, and he pulled up a chair.

When he found out that I was an American, he beamed. In his limited English, he said, "Oh! How I love America!" I could barely understand him, but he spoke with such love and emotion that I clung to every word he said, afraid that I might miss something. He told me that he comes to the American base in Gaeta to see the two flags side by side: the Italian flag and Old Glory, flying together. Every time he sees an American flag, he lowers his head and prays, and he always ends his prayer with: "God bless America, and God remember Italy, too!"

He grew up here in Gaeta, and his family suffered during the war. He told me how the Germans took everything his family had, including their home. They nearly starved to death. He dug into trash cans to look for food for his family. Some of them were sick, and it seemed as if they would die. My new friend said that he prayed to God to save them—and God sent the American troops. The way he saw it, the troops didn't come to invade Italy, but to save him and his family.

The old man trembled as he talked, pausing several times to fight back the tears. I was trying hard to fight back my own tears, but it was a losing battle.

A young navy doctor saw him digging in the trash and went home with him, bringing food and medicine to his family. "I was much too sick already," said the old man. "The medicine didn't help me, and for three days I was in a coma." When he woke up, his father had told him that the navy doctor had never left his side during those three days. That doctor saved his life. His father wept, saying, "I will always love America, because my son was dead, and America came and brought him back to me."

It would be many years before this man even learned the name of the doctor who had saved his life, but he never forgot him, nor did he ever stop loving his beloved America.

After he grew up and married, he went to visit his beautiful America. He visited Washington, and there he saw some young people burning Old Glory. His voice was shaking. His emotions grew raw. He looked at me with huge tears in his eyes, and told me how it hurt his heart to see that beautiful old flag being burned. He touched his wife's hand and asked her to stay where she was. This Italian man walked over to the Americans who were burning the flag and asked them, "Why?" They began to explain their protest, and he simply said, "But why must you burn Old Glory? She stands for all that I love, and I owe her my life." He shared his story with them, and their heads hung down. They extinguished the flames, gave him the burned remains of the flag and walked away.

By this time my face was soaked with tears. His story bridged the differences I had been seeing in our two worlds. I saw the beauty of the countryside with new eyes. I don't remember the name of the man who forever changed my heart and touched my spirit, but not a day goes by that I don't think about him. Every time I drive to our base in Italy, I see our two flags flying, side by side. I bow my head, and I pray, and I always end my prayer with: "God bless America, and God . . . remember Italy, too!"

Stacy Smith Kirchheiner

A Quiet Road

Who shall set a limit to the influence of a human being?

Ralph Waldo Emerson

I like to read signs. They hint at the flavor of places. Small, easy-to-miss signs posted on the highway have informative and sometimes inventive names. Rivers and lakes, such as Clear Boggy River and Coffeepot Lake, intrigue me. Other signs with names like Terrebonne Parrish and Muleshoe, Texas, offer insights to their distinct regions. I look with longing at the brown highway signs that state, "Historical Marker, 1 mile," because we're always flying along to our destination and can't stop. But I'd like to pull over and contemplate an old battlefield, now silent and peaceful.

Naturally, I glanced at the green sign as we turned onto one of Alabama's state highways and read, "Johnny Michael Spann Memorial Highway." After a second of wondering why that name sounded so familiar, I realized with a jolt where I'd heard the name: on the news. Johnny Michael Spann, a CIA officer, was killed during the bloody prison uprising in Mazar-e Sharif in our war on terrorism in Afghanistan. I remembered the reporters, squinting in the glaring light reflecting off the barren landscape, and the almost musical lilt of the name Mazar-e Sharif rolling off their tongues, followed by the phrase, ". . . the first American combat death."

I picked up the walkie-talkie and pushed the button. Ahead of me in his little blue car, my husband reached over and grabbed his walkie-talkie. "Did you see the name of this road?" I asked.

A crackle of static sounded, then he said, "No."

"It's the Johnny Michael Spann Memorial Highway."

After a second he said, "Wow."

He didn't say anything else. Neither did I. We didn't need to. My husband is a pilot in the Air Force Reserve. We knew firsthand the rewards and risks of serving our country. We were silent—a respectful stillness—as we cruised down the highway.

I'd never thought about why we named roads after people. I'd always pictured a famous politician or successful businessperson when I saw a sign and I didn't recognize the name. But naming a highway after a patriot struck me as appropriate. After all, the roads that crisscross our country symbolize our freedom to choose our own course and move unchecked across town or across the country as we live our lives and pursue our dreams. In fact, we were an example of that freedom in action. With my husband leading, I brought up the rear in the minivan loaded with two kids, two dogs and miscellaneous toys, luggage and houseplants, as we skimmed along the freeway. We'd left Oklahoma's rolling hills dotted with scrub oak and headed toward middle Georgia for a new job, a government service position linked to his part-time job as an Air Force Reservist.

On that overcast Sunday, I studied the semirural road

and wondered: *Why this road? Why not a busy commercial district, at the heart of town?* I contemplated the modest, scattered homes set back from the road. Smoke curled up from a few chimneys on that chilly day, and I pictured people reading the Sunday paper with a cup of coffee. Then it seemed exactly right to name this road for Spann, a place where people went about their business, quietly lived their lives and made their choices. Spann had joined a company of people who, beginning with the Revolutionary War's Battles of Lexington and Concord and running through time to a prison near Mazar-e Sharif, had died giving Americans the ability to pursue life, liberty and happiness.

We followed the gentle curves of the road past the houses and between the tall pines. I wondered if Spann or his family lived on this road. It didn't matter, I decided, as the road unfurled before us. This calm stretch of road in Alabama showed what our troops were fighting and dying for: the opportunity to live our lives in quiet freedom.

Sara Rosett

The Call Home

My husband is in the army. As part of an infantry unit at the 101st Airborne (Air Assault) Division in Fort Campbell, Kentucky, he left for the war in Iraq on March 2, 2003, but he assured me that he would call as often as he could.

Three days after he left, he called me from Camp New York in Kuwait. I received calls from him on a regular basis for about a month. Then, he told me that he was leaving Camp New York. He couldn't tell me where he was going, but he knew he wouldn't be able to call me for a month or more. Not only was I worried about where he was going, but, more so, what he was going to be doing.

A few weeks went by, and I had heard nothing. Since I hadn't been part of the military world for very long, I was getting very worried. I talked to wives of his fellow soldiers, and no one had heard anything. I watched the news all the time, and the war just seemed to be getting more and more intense and violent.

One night, about a month since the last time he had called, I was lying in bed, crying my eyes out and praying with all my heart. "Please, God, just let me know he is okay. Please! I have to know he is okay!" I cried all night and got very little sleep. The next day, I was driving down the interstate when my cell phone rang. It was a number that I didn't recognize, and my heart raced as I answered it. "Hello? . . . Hello?" I answered.

"Hi, baby!" The familiar voice on the other end was his!

"Oh, my gosh! How are you?" Questions were racing through my head, flooding my mind.

He said, "I'm okay. I found this satellite phone in a field, and it worked. I love you and I'm okay."

"I love you, too! I miss you so much!" I replied. And then the phone went silent and nothing else. I sat there and waited for him to call back, but he didn't. I knew that was the answer to my prayer. All I wanted to know was that he was okay. I thought to myself, *What are the odds of his finding a satellite phone in the middle of the desert?* I didn't hear from him for about twenty more days, but that didn't bother me because I knew he was alive and okay.

He is home safe now. To this day, I still sit in awe of God and his miraculous ways.

C. Boggs

Pregnancy

You must do the thing you think you cannot do.

Eleanor Roosevelt

Pregnancy is never easy. When your spouse is away, it can be even more difficult. For my new family, 1999 was a bustling year. Not only had I married my husband, George, a sergeant in the U.S. Army, but we were also expecting our first child.

Several months into our marriage and into my pregnancy, George came up on orders to go to Kuwait for a one-year tour. I was devastated. Although I wanted him to be at home with me, I knew that he had a job to do and that he was needed in Kuwait. This is the life of a military wife.

As my due date approached, it became overwhelmingly obvious that George was not going to be granted his request for leave. I would have to give birth without him. My due date came and went. At a routine examination, I was told that I was in labor and that I needed to get to the hospital immediately. On the drive to the hospital I fought with uncooperative DSN lines, trying unsuccessfully to

get a hook flash to Camp Doha where George was stationed. My husband was not even going to know that his
daughter was being born.

I also made a quick phone call to my mother, who was
at home with my younger sister. Once at the hospital, my
labor progressed quite rapidly, and my older sister, who
had accompanied me, manned the camera. I wanted
George to be able to share in the experience of birth, even
if he could not be there in person.

We were well on our way when the door to the delivery
room flew open—and in walked George. Fate had smiled
upon him, and, at the last moment, he had been granted
his leave pass. He had flown for over sixteen hours on an
AMC flight from Kuwait. After arriving at my mother's
house and getting word that his daughter was being born,
he quickly rushed to the hospital. George joined me for
one last push, and we welcomed our daughter Kaylee into
the world, together.

Every nurse on the labor-and-delivery floor was in
tears at this act of love. By the next morning the entire
hospital knew about the soldier who, by the grace of God,
flew across the world in the nick of time.

Michele Putman

My Nurse Angel

You have to leave room in life to dream.

Buffy Sainte-Marie

The Georgia air was thick as the young mother-to-be and her husband entered the hospital. The girl was eight months pregnant and running a fever.

A nurse with warm brown skin and a caring smile ushered them into the examination room and sent the nervous young soldier into the waiting area so the staff could examine his wife. After the exam, the nurse explained to the girl that she had a virus, but she and the baby would be fine if she got some rest.

The young woman with the bulging belly began to cry softly. You see, she was a newlywed, married only six months when she found out that she would be a mother. In addition, she and her new husband had left their hometown, the place where they were both born and raised, to begin a new life in the military. They were young, inexperienced and new to the ways of the army.

As the girl cried, the nurse spoke, her voice tender yet stern. "Now, you listen here, baby. You gonna be just fine, and, in about two weeks, you gonna be up here to have that baby, and I'll be right here with you. Don't you worry none now. I'll be right here."

The girl blinked and dried her eyes. "But how will you know I'm here?" she asked. "Do you work here on the labor-and-delivery floor?"

"No, honey. I work at the other end of the hall. Don't you worry about that. I'll just know you're here. Now, you go on home. Make Daddy take good care of you, and I'll see you soon enough."

This gave comfort to the young army wife, and she thought several times of the woman with the warm smile. The days ticked by until it was time to go to the hospital again. Her labor progressed and she continued with natural labor, breathing and being coached by her husband. As the pain increased, there, alongside one of the birth attendants, she saw the same warm, caring lady with the pretty smile.

"I told you I'd be here, now, didn't I?" she asked.

The young mother was so very happy to see a familiar face, as she didn't know anyone who was helping her, nor did she have any idea which doctor would actually deliver the baby. A pain soon gripped her and her special nurse helped, coaxing and soothing her along with her husband. She praised the laboring girl and assured her that she wouldn't leave until the hard work was finished.

After a few hours of labor, it was time to be wheeled into the delivery room, leaving the nurse behind.

In the delivery room, the baby quickly entered this world; the young man and his bride were so awed by their new baby girl! Perfect! So healthy and strong, and, like every baby, a miracle from the Maker of us all. The overwhelming emotions of parenthood overtook the couple as they watched and held their newborn baby.

Soon, the baby began to nurse and the girl's mother arrived to help care for the new family.

The young mother asked one of the nurses about the nurse who had helped her so much, but none of the nurses knew who she was talking about.

As I talked with my husband Rick about writing this story, I mentioned that special nurse, the one who had coached me through that tough exam and childbirth, the one I had never been able to thank properly.

He looked at me and paused a moment. Very softly he said, "Lisa, I surely remember your labor, but I never saw her."

Today, I am an army wife of seventeen years, a mother of three and a registered nurse of eleven years. We have lived on three continents, met many incredible people and have had many wonderful experiences. We have been blessed by God, as we strive to serve him and bring honor to him in all that we do each and every day. He continues to provide us with all that we need, just like he did fifteen years ago with my nurse angel.

Lisa Cobb

The Calm During the Storm

*The only thing that makes life possible is perma-
nent, intolerant uncertainty; not knowing what
comes next.*

Ursula K. Le Guin

I have always gone to wave farewell to my husband when
he departs on a mission. I stand behind the approachment
line on the ground as he taxis his aircraft, and watch his
crew wave back out of one of the open aircraft windows. My
husband is a pilot of an MH-53 Special Operations helicopter in the air force, and saying good-bye is emotional.
My parting words to him are, "Please be safe." His response
is a smile and, "I'll be home soon." This is our ritual.

On May 21, 2002, he was called to action. Nothing can
prepare you for the bravery you must summon when you
get a phone call telling you a mission is under way. My
husband called to say he was departing and to tell me he
loved me. He would be airborne before I could make it to
wave farewell.

I had kissed him good-bye just hours before, but when
he left for work it was for an ordinary training flight.

Special Operations mostly operates at night, and I told
him I would try to stay up and wait for him. I had not
known there was a chance I would not see him until he
returned from a "real life" mission.

As with all Special Ops Pave Low helicopter missions, I
didn't have a clue where my husband was going or when
he would be back. The duration of the mission is sometimes unknown and often is classified.

As I later learned, what began as an ordinary day saw
one of the longest missions ever flown by a helicopter
crew. My husband was involved in what is believed to be
the longest over-water rescue ever conducted: a journey
of approximately thirteen hours, covering more than nine
hundred miles round trip, to rescue passengers aboard a
troubled yacht in the Atlantic Ocean. The crew flew
overnight, with winds gusting more than fifty miles an
hour and waves hitting the helicopter. The mission was
successful. The helicopter crew returned home safely, but
was exhausted.

I learned this not from my humble husband, but from
the media accounts of the mission. The crews of the
MH-53 helicopters never seek credit. For them, gratifica-
tion comes from the success of a mission. It is rare to hear
anyone boast about their accomplishments in Special Ops.

When I read the newspaper reports and saw the photos, I was on my knees to God, grateful that I would be
reunited with my husband.

Now, my husband is no longer on a peacetime mission.
Our country is at war, liberating another country. When
my husband returns home safely, I will be on my knees
before God again, thankful and relieved.

The opportunity to say farewell is meaningful, but the
chance to say "hello" means everything.

Kathy Oberhaus

Miracle Wallet

We are here not only to learn about love, but to also support and teach our fellow travelers on this journey.

Mary Manin Morressey

As a military wife of sixteen years, I stay quite busy and have little time for reflection. As a mother of three children and a nurse with a small teaching job, you can guess I don't often think about times past. Over the years, we have traveled and lived in many different places, and there have been many people who have touched our lives in ways that I will never forget. Despite hectic schedules, sometimes a story needs to be shared with others.

We were stationed at Fort Campbell outside of Clarksville, Tennessee, only three hours away from our hometown of Florence, Alabama. My husband was on temporary duty in Africa, and I thought I would take my two girls home for a few days to give them some time with their grandparents. I needed a break, and four-year-old Bethany and ten-year-old Sydney would enjoy the trip.

One crisp, clear spring morning, we set out for home in our small station wagon. After an hour on the road, I pulled off the interstate at Brentwood and stopped at a gas station. A while later, I needed to stop again to buy some snacks for the girls. I reached for my wallet to get change . . . and it was gone. *No!*

I thought about the gas station where I had stopped earlier. *Okay,* I thought, trying to calm myself in front of the children, *think! Into the station . . . bought juice after the bathroom . . . then out to the car . . . strapped Bethany in . . . The wallet! I put it on top of the car beside the luggage rack! Oh no!* I already knew the answer but stole a quick look at the top of the car to confirm it wasn't still there.

I did a quick mental inventory. As a military dependent, my identification card was vital to my survival in everyday life, especially with my husband gone. Also, my Social Security card, driver's license and my adopted daughter's green card were in there! I couldn't easily replace that! It was the longest drive to Florence, and I reluctantly told my in-laws about the wallet I left on top of my car.

My father-in-law and I hurried to call the Brentwood police. They hadn't heard of anyone turning in my wallet but promised to look around the gas station and ask the attendants there if anyone had turned it in.

I knew in my mind that there was little to no possibility of my wallet being found, much less returned to me, as I had no current address or phone numbers in it, thanks to our many military moves.

The next day, the phone rang. The girl said she was calling from the Blockbuster Video in Florence. She asked my name and if I had a Blockbuster card in my wallet.

"Yes," I answered, very puzzled.

"Someone has found your wallet and is waiting here at our store. Can you come? They'll be outside waiting for you."

"Of course! I'll be right there!" I scrambled out the door, totally confused, amazed and happy. As I pulled up into the parking lot, I saw a station wagon with three people sitting in the back with the hatch up, two women and a man. I stepped out of the car, and the younger lady came up to me and asked, "Are you Lisa?"

It seems the couple and her mother were on a day trip from Tennessee to the Dismals, a nature park in northwest Alabama. As her mom said, "I have this bad smokin' habit, and I guess the good Lord's tryin' to tell me somethin' 'cause I caught myself on fire as we pulled the car back onto the interstate from Brentwood. I pulled over to jump out and brush off the ashes, and as I was walking behind the car I saw your wallet."

At this point she scolded me. "Honey, you need to promise me to put your address and phone number in your wallet 'cause we couldn't find anything but that Blockbuster card to possibly help us find you!"

This family went out of their way to find the Blockbuster Video with the hope of the store being able to find me. I hadn't used that card, having gotten it in Florence on a previous visit, but the account had a phone number! Luckily for me, the most logical route from Tennessee to the Dismals goes right through . . . Florence, Alabama.

Of course, I thanked them profusely, but I still regret that I never thought to get their address. That kind act reminded me that there are truly honest people in our world, no matter how bleak things seem when we read the newspaper.

So, to that certain family of three, you seemed more like angels to me. If you are reading this story, I thank you again for your honesty, caring and kindness.

And to the mom in the group: my phone number and address are now in my wallet, updated with every move!

Lisa Cobb

A Soldier, Someone's Child

Healing is not done in the mind or by the powers of the intellect; it is done in the heart.

H. B. Jeffery

We stood there awkwardly. He wore a camouflage uniform, looking like an adolescent playing grown-up. Suddenly, he reached out and put his arms around me. He clung to me as if I was his lifeline. This man-child needed compassion, a human touch and the reassurance that someone cared. He had seen things that we baby boomers had tried so hard to shelter our children from. He was only nineteen.

I first met this young man when I was assigned to help him and his wife take advantage of all the resources available to them as new parents. Instead of living in base housing, they inhabited a tiny apartment in a decrepit neighborhood. Her family lived out of state and she had no friends. Although he was often present during my home visits, he barely spoke and usually retreated to their bedroom. I had the feeling that he didn't really want me to be there.

Over the next several months, I made biweekly visits to their home. The young wife had overcome many challenges. She had been alone during most of her pregnancy while her husband went through basic training. While pregnant, she had been involved in a serious automobile accident and required hospitalization. They were now coping with the harshest reality of military life: He was deploying to Iraq.

She confided that he had recently lost his mother, still in her thirties, to cancer, and that he had not had the opportunity to grieve. He had never known his dad and had no other immediate family members. Additionally, in his early teens, he had converted to the Muslim faith. The war in Iraq would be a test for him: of his fitness to serve in the American military in a conflict that would test both his faith and his patriotism.

When he deployed, his young bride and their infant went to live with her parents. Six months later, I received a message stating that he had returned home and that she had called to request continuing services from our agency. She had also indicated that she wished for me to again be her caseworker. I readily agreed.

The first visit to their home was somewhat strained. I could feel the tension in the air. When the soldier left the room, his wife confided that she was suffering from depression and that worrying about her made his stress level even higher. He was sleeping fitfully and had become moody, but never violent. He had also attempted to talk to her of the things he had experienced in combat—the sights, the sounds, the smells. She wanted to be there for him, to empathize, but she didn't know what to say or do.

We discussed the need for her to follow up with her primary-care provider and to request a mental-health referral. We devised a safety plan for dealing with episodes of anxiety and stress that could put any of the family members in jeopardy. We especially discussed the impact of stress on their relationship with each other and on the welfare of their child. We discussed resources available and agreed to weekly home visits.

It was now three weeks after my initial reassignment to the case. The young soldier was home during the visit and when I asked him nonthreatening questions, he answered in more than his customary curt responses. We discussed stress, grief and depression, and how they were all intertwined.

When his wife left the room to change the baby, he leaned over to tell me how worried he was about her. He began to talk, and I listened. As he talked, his eyes became moist. At times his voice shook. He spoke of his love for America, his love for the military and his love for his family. He spoke of the need to be strong for his wife and baby, and how unsure of himself he felt at times. He spoke of what he had seen and heard. He spoke of his love for his mother.

I told him about post-traumatic stress disorder and how normal the responses he felt were under the circumstances. He agreed to at least consider counseling, and I gave him some referral information for free clinics. His wife returned to the room and joined the discussion. She agreed to take advantage of available childcare resources so that she could discuss her situation with her physician, uninterrupted. I offered to accompany her if she wished. She also spoke of her desire to continue her education, to get a GED, to go to college. He spoke of his desire to send their daughter to college someday. Together they were focusing on a future filled with promise.

The home visit was over, and it was time for me to wrap up what had proven to be a long and emotionally draining day. However, I couldn't leave—not just yet. This soldier, with the tracks of tears still on his cheeks, needed a hug. He needed warmth and compassion. So, for just a moment, I put aside professional boundaries. For just a few minutes, I imagined what my own grown son would be experiencing under the same circumstances. For just a few minutes, I gave him the hugs and encouragement that perhaps his mother would have given if she were here.

Then, with a heart full of hope and the tracks of my own tears staining my cheeks, I completed my paperwork as a home health nurse and drove home.

I checked the answering machine. There were no messages. I checked the mailbox. Finally! A long-awaited letter from my husband, who is serving in Iraq. I, too, am a military wife.

Elizabeth Martin, R.N.

All in a Day's Work

No one is where he is by accident, and chance plays no part in God's plan.

A Course in Miracles

My husband and my son are both serving in Iraq. Bill, my husband, is in the California National Guard, and Kyle, my son, is with the army's 4th Infantry Division.

Listening to some Christian songs one evening in my kitchen I was reminded of my soldiers, who I miss and pray for every day. I sat down right there on the kitchen floor and began to talk to God, asking him to please wrap his loving arms around them both. I asked him to protect them, guide them, watch over them and bring them home safely to me. I begged him to bring them together, if it was his will. For half an hour, I just spoke my heart.

At about four the next morning, Bill called me and told me an incredible story. While I was at home praying for my boys, Bill had just finished his mission to Mosul and crossed the border into Kuwait. He was returning safely to base camp, and, on the way, they stopped in Tikrit. As they traveled in their convoy, one of the trucks ran over a crude Iraqi bomb. It created a huge fireball and one of the HET (heavy equipment transporter) vehicles was fully engulfed in flames. The driver was injured, but no one was killed. Their convoy stopped and pulled over on the side of the road, and there was a fight with enemy soldiers. One of the vehicles sent word to area military units that they were under attack. By the time support arrived, the situation was under control.

Then Bill turned a corner and walked right into Kyle! The message had been received by the 4th ID, and our son, who was stationed in southern Tikrit, heard the message. He jumped in a Humvee and headed north, because he knew that this was his dad's unit. Kyle had been frantically looking for Bill, and when he found him, they gave each other the biggest hugs they had ever exchanged.

I don't think that either of them will forget that moment. My husband and son may have been far away, but they were close to my heart. Bill and Kyle were with each other, as they had been in my prayers, and God was with us all.

Liz Rae

2

I MISS YOU SO

Two persons' love in one another is the future good which they aid one another to unfold.

Charlotte Perkins Gilman

A Navy Wife's Prayer

How often we've stood on dark flight lines and piers . . .
"I love you," "I'll miss you" whispered through tears.
During long separations, in peacetime, at war . . .
my nights filled with dreams of this man I adore.
With only my memories to hold close at night . . .
I live for the day God returns my sunlight.
Yes, life goes on when your loved one's at sea . . .
but the ache never leaves, the fear stays with me.
Dear Lord, I need your guidance, your love . . .
help me be brave, keep your watch from above.
Hold my dear one so safe in your heart and your hand . . .
bring him home to his family . . . this hero . . . my man.
Of us, Lord, I pray he'll be filled with such pride . . .
of how we carried on without him by our side.
Please, help time fly quickly and soon I will hold . . .
the hand of the man whose eyes chase the cold.
Whose voice brings delight, whose touch eases pain.
How will I ever say "Farewell" again?
With your help, dear God, I'll try to stay strong . . .
and pray that his time here at home will be long.
Still, "I know that the navy will need him," I sigh . . .
but we'll face it together, Dear Lord, you and I.

Sue Ellen Groseclose-Combs

Picture the Waiting

Hope is the feeling you have that the feeling you have isn't permanent.

Jean Kerr

In my grandmother's home, there is a framed image of a young girl with long blonde hair sitting on a high, rocky ledge overlooking the sea. The intense colors of the darkening, star-filled night sky mix with the deep blues of the calm ocean. She wears a white dress that glows in the light of the moon. Her tiny, sharp-featured face is sullen and sad, and her arms wind loosely around her legs. Her eyes gaze out longingly over the sea, but she cannot see what lies many miles away.

On September 18, 1917, my grandmother was sitting alone in her tiny one-room shack holding a newborn baby girl. The only things that adorned the walls of her home were a medicine chest that her grandfather had made for her and the picture of a young girl looking out toward places unseen.

Attached to the picture's corner was a letter. It read:

Dearest Lenny,

Woodrow called me to serve and you know I had to go. I'll send back my pay so that you and Grace will be taken care of. Pray for my comrades and me, and give Grace a big kiss. I'll be home soon.

With all my love,
Jim

Her Jim was a man who never wrote, and this note was a surprise to her. She folded it neatly several times and tucked it safely in her apron pocket.

She did what she had to do, but the nights were long as she walked and rocked her young, crying daughter. A tiny radio foretold the possibility of war, and, on October 23, 1917, her throat tightened and her heart pounded as the news reported that "the first American Doughboys were stepping onto foreign soil."

Grandma knew Grandpa was one of them.

Within two months, Grandma received Grandpa's first check and was able to pay up the bills. An enclosed letter said that her husband had made arrangements for his checks to be delivered directly to her the first of each month. That comforted her because she knew as long as the checks came, Grandpa was okay.

As the months wore on, Grandma was grateful that the army hadn't visited her door. Neighbors and friends were already dealing with the loss of husbands, brothers, uncles and children. Her own sister received an official letter that stated her husband was missing in action.

Grace started walking at six months. Grandma packaged a picture of their beautiful daughter stepping lightly across the floor with a long family letter. Sealing it with a kiss, she wrote, "Miss you much," on the envelope and mailed it off. After several weeks, the letter and picture were returned with the handwritten message, "Unable to locate soldier," scrawled across its front.

Grandma tucked the letter in her apron pocket and slumped into the big, overstuffed blue chair that faced the picture. Her tears flowed as she stared into the picture and placed herself into the body of the girl. She felt her hollow heart skipping beats as the Atlantic slammed her soul.

Taking a deep breath, Grandma prayed for all the men who were lost and scared this night. With a strong "Amen," a calm came over her. She realized that the young woman in the picture was also waiting for her love to come home. Suddenly, she didn't feel so alone. She had someone to wait with.

When the months had rolled into the second year of America's involvement in World War I, Grandma had settled into a quiet routine. Grace was walking and talking, the house was immaculate, and life went on. Grandpa's checks were arriving each month and she told no one about the returned letter.

On the eleventh hour of the eleventh day of the eleventh month of 1918, a cease-fire went into effect for all combatants. The war was over, but before the official armistice was declared, 9 million people had died on the battlefield, and the world was forever changed.

On April 6, 1919, Aunt Martha handed Grandma a letter that she had received by accident. It was official army issue, stamps, seals and all. She carried it inside and sat heavily in the chair. She called Grace to her lap and cradled her close as she opened the envelope with trembling, cold hands. As she pulled the letter out of the envelope it fell to the floor. Two words jumped out at her: *coming* and *home*. Retrieving the letter, she smoothed it out and started reading. Jim's unit would be coming home on April 7, 1919, at 9:00 A.M. That was tomorrow!

The next morning, she dressed Grace and herself in their finest attire, and they arrived at the dock at 8:30 A.M. The ship was already there, and she placed herself at the end of the gangplank. A serviceman came over and asked her whom she was there to see. She told him but then asked, "Why?"

"We have special messages for some of the wives. Let me see if you're one of them." With that, he walked away.

Soon cheers were heard from the ship and men of all ages were running down the plank toward waiting arms. As the last of the men were embraced, Grandma found herself manless. Swallowing hard, she squeezed Grace's hand tightly and scanned the ship. Suddenly, the serviceman appeared at the top of the gangplank with a handful of envelopes and a high-ranking officer. As they descended the plank, Grandma stepped back and caressed Grace's hair. She closed her eyes and started to pray.

"Mrs. Adams?"

"Yes," a weak voice sprung up from behind the crowd.

"We are sorry to inform you that Robert J. Adams was killed while in the service of his country. . . ."

Grandma's heart fell almost as far as the just-widowed wife's did.

"Mrs. Becker?"

Another note was passed on.

By the tenth passing, Grandma turned and started the long walk home.

"Mrs. Creed?"

Grandma's heart stopped.

"Don't you want to go home with your husband?" the voice said.

She turned slowly to greet the face that asked the question. Grandma fell to her knees and sobbed into Grace's dress as Grandpa knelt beside her and hugged his family for the first time in almost a year and a half.

After they tucked Grace into bed, Grandpa found Grandma sitting in the big blue chair staring at the picture. For the first time, it looked to her as if her friend in the painting was smiling.

Candace Carteen

Letters of Hope

"Love is patient and kind. . . . Love never gives up; and its faith, hope and patience never fail" (1 Corinthians 13:4). Our Gran Lindsay who now lives in Burlington, Ontario, has this scripture printed on a magnet on her fridge. To some visitors it is only a magnet to our family it is a gentle reminder of a cherished family story.

It all began with a message in the town newspaper: "LINDSAY: Darling I am well . . . Hope you and the children are fine." The year was 1943. A ham radio operator had picked up the fragmented message and directed it to the small-town newspaper.

Martha Lindsay had waited thirteen long months for any glimmer of hope, that her husband William Lindsay had survived the sinking of the H.M.S. *Exeter* on March 1, 1942. Holding onto that hope, she waited for word from the Red Cross. The days turned into weeks, and no word from the Red Cross. Martha did her best to stay busy with the children, always keeping William in her prayers. Finally one afternoon, the Red Cross contacted her with the news that she had been praying for: A William Lindsay had been located and was presently a prisoner of war.

Martha's heart soared. William was alive; she had never given up hope. Martha was instructed to write messages to William. She was to write no more than twenty-five words on a plain white postcard and then forward them to Geneva. Only one postcard a month was permitted. Martha wrote to William of the antics of their children Billy and Catherine, who had been babies the last time he saw them. She did her best to express her love and devotion to him on the tiny white postcards. In twenty-five words she kept reminding him that he was loved. Two and a half agonizing years passed without receiving a reply, but still Martha's faith and hope never faltered.

One September morning in 1945, as Martha was getting ready to take the children to school, the mailman delivered a small scrap of paper through the mail slot. It had no envelope and no stamp. As she turned the paper over, her heart began to pound and her eyes filled with tears as she recognized William's handwriting: "Martha, I've been released. I'm coming home."

On a beautiful day in October 1945, William Lindsay returned home to his family. After their tears of joy had subsided, Martha asked him if he had received her letters, and she learned sadly, that not one had found its way to the camp.

Shortly after William's arrival home, there was a knock at the door. Martha answered to find a young sailor standing in the doorway.

"Excuse me, are you Martha Lindsay?"

"Yes, I am," she replied.

"Was your husband a prisoner of war?"

"Yes," she whispered.

With a tear in his eye, he introduced himself. "My name is William Lindsay. I too was a prisoner of war." Very slowly he reached into his pocket and handed her thirty tiny white postcards tied in a ribbon.

"I received one every month. They were the glimmer of hope that helped me survive. From the bottom of my heart, thank you." Very gently, Martha placed them back into his hands where he held them to his heart.

"Love is patient and kind. . . . Love never gives up; and its faith, hope and patience never fail" (1 Corinthians 13:4).

Shelley McEwan

A Chain of Love

I do not teach children. I give them joy.

Isadora Duncan

I had read many books and articles about dealing with a spouse's deployment and keeping kids happy and positive during those trying times, and came up with our "Chain of Love." Every day, my son and I would cut a piece of colorful construction paper into five large strips. On one side of the strip, we would write the date and the number of days his daddy has been gone. On the other side, we would write how we felt that day. Our messages to Daddy have ranged from, "We love you and miss you," "We hope that Daddy is being careful and staying safe," to "We are having a bad day today, and we wish Daddy was here to comfort us."

By linking them together, we have connected all these strips into a paper chain that hangs in the living room of our house. We started on one end, near the entrance of our home, and are continuing around until the chain meets its beginning. This is something that my son looks forward to and really enjoys doing. We have made it an everyday ritual. After breakfast every morning, we choose the next color strip and write our message to Daddy. We have taken pictures of our chain and sent them periodically to Jim so he can see that our Chain of Love grows every day that he is gone. He enjoys the photos and is looking forward to coming home and reading every message we wrote for him.

At the beginning, it was hard for my son to express how he felt. However, as the days have gone by, it has become easier for him. He sees this as an opportunity to talk to his daddy and tell him how he feels, especially because the phone calls are so scarce. The chain starts at the entrance of our home and will end there—and on the day that he walks through that front door, it will demonstrate every tear, smile, hug and kiss that he missed while he was serving proudly for our freedom.

He will know that our separation did not break our Chain of Love.

Tammy C. Logan

Deployed

An effort made for the happiness of others lifts us above ourselves.

Lydia Marie Child

When my husband deployed, we were given an address where we could mail our letters and packages, but the army initially told us to hold off sending anything until the guys were "settled." A few weeks into the deployment, the colonel's wife called me and told me that I could tell the other wives that we had a green light to send mail. After I shared the news, I could practically smell the pencil lead burning through reams of paper all through the Fort Campbell community!

I put together two boxes of mostly snack food. Knowing my husband is a real health nut, I wanted to make sure I was sending stuff that he would eat because he will go without a meal if it is too high in fat and calories. I waited until the girls were up from their naps so everyone would be in good spirits, and we went off to the local post office.

In all my past experiences, I've always had to wait in line, and I knew that, with the kids—Hannah is two and a half, and Charlotte is one—it would be interesting. Once I opened the door to the post office, I saw just what I had expected: a long line! I started to panic. Like most moms, I was praying that the girls would stay happy long enough to get to the head of the line so that we could get in and out without some type of tantrum.

Most of the people in line were military wives holding boxes addressed to APO addresses. Most boxes were decorated with stickers and children's artwork. Instantly, I got a lump in my throat. The man at the counter yelled, "If you're mailing something APO, don't forget your customs form!" The group started to scramble for the necessary forms. I was the only one in the group who had brought children, and, as I said, you have to be brave to take your kids to the post office when you are guaranteed a wait.

When I heard about the customs form that had to be filled out, my face must have shown my stress. I was holding two huge boxes, trying to keep the girls entertained, and looking around frantically for the necessary forms, when my angel appeared.

A very distinguished older gentleman in a three-piece suit came up to me and said in a very kind voice, "Would you like me to hold your baby so you can fill out your forms?"

I looked him over and said, "You must be a grandpa. That would be so helpful, but my Charlotte won't really let anyone hold her. We can give it a shot. . . ." I handed Charlotte over, and she was actually very content! While he held her in his arms, he took the American flag pin off his lapel and put it on her coat.

As I busied myself with the paperwork, he spoke to both my girls: "Your daddy is very brave to be a soldier, and all of us here sure do appreciate him leaving you two beauties to take care of us."

I finished filling out my forms, and, when I took Charlotte back, before I had a chance to thank him, he said, "God bless you and your family. Thank you for making the tremendous sacrifices that you do to ensure all our safety, and God bless America."

After that, he left the post office. Tears welled up in my eyes. Not many people thank me for anything, let alone help a single mommy in a situation like that.

Being in the post office with a bunch of women all holding onto their packages for their loved ones is something that I will never forget.

Naomi Stanton

Silent Survivors of the Vietnam War

Learn to let go. That is the only key to happiness.

Buddha

1962. I remember when I first realized I loved Bill. It was Army/Navy Weekend. I arrived in Annapolis, and Bill wasn't at the station to meet me, so I waited. I watched him approach, and I felt something connecting us as he drew near.

1964. He graduated in June, and we married the very next week.

1965. The Vieques cruise. I learned I was pregnant while he was gone.

1966. His first tour in Vietnam started in January. In March, Sarah was born.

1967. He returned in April.

1969. He left for Vietnam again in June. On the day he left, I learned that I was pregnant again.

1970. In January, our daughter Mitty was born. He was still in Vietnam. The next morning, two men in uniform got off the elevator and spoke to my aunt. I could see them from my hospital bed. I knew who they were. My aunt became upset, and a nurse hurried into my room and took the baby away. I waited. Every military wife dreads the day two uniformed men and a priest come to the door. My Bill was gone.

1994. I decided to pursue a doctorate in psychology. As a student, while reading literature on post-traumatic stress disorder, I found little research concerning the wives of Vietnam veterans. As a widow of that war, I wondered about the other women, and I thought more about myself and my own responses. Dormant feelings were roused, and my stoicism crumbled.

Bill had been away for more than half of our five-year marriage. I was angry with him for getting himself killed, and, instead of grieving, I denied how much his death had affected me. When he died, I was only twenty-seven years old, too young to be a widow. I remarried twice, but there was a Bill-shaped hole that no one could fill. Competing with a dead man must have been difficult for my ex-husbands.

Memorial Day weekend. My two grown daughters and I went to Washington, D.C., to visit the Vietnam Memorial. Their father's name is on that wall. The purpose of our trip was to acquaint them with the man they had never known.

We visited his school, the base of his first duty assignment and the first apartment we lived in after our marriage. One of Bill's closest friends was the base commander at Quantico Marine Corps Base, and we were able to visit the base quarters that had been our last home together. The girls and I heard many stories about their dad. After nearly twenty-five years, I finally was able and willing to tell them about their father and answer their questions.

Before we left for the return trip home, we took one last walk to the wall. Sarah, who had been three when her father died and not allowed to attend the funeral, told me that she felt she had finally been allowed to honor his life. Mitty, who had been born the day before her father's death, reached out and touched his name. In the softest voice, she said, "This isn't just a name anymore. This is my daddy."

The sense of loss has never gone away, but it has blended into the fabric of my life, creating a complicated pattern of bereavement, courage, strength and joy. I took many pictures while we were in Washington. My favorite is a photograph of Bill's panel. You can see his name and my reflection, joined together on the shining surface.

Sally B. Griffis

The Phone Call

Tact is, after all, a kind of mind reading.

Sarah Orne Jewett

"Is this Mrs. Smith?" An unidentified male voice was on the phone. I cautiously responded. Was this the phone call I had been dreading since March? For a moment, I thought I was going to be sick. Then the loveliest words I have ever heard came through the receiver: "Smith, your wife's on the phone."

At 5:20 A.M., on April 18, my heart leapt to my throat. I had not heard my husband's voice since February 16. For a moment, I wondered if he would sound the same. I wondered if I remembered his voice at all.

The news channel I am now addicted to had not reported anything from his brigade in a week. Immediately, what seemed to be a thousand questions flew through my head. *Where are you? How are you? Have you been able to shower? Are you eating? Do you miss me? Why has it taken you so long to call?*

Intellectually speaking, I knew why he had not called. Jay was in a war zone. However, this fact had not prevented me from embarking upon the longest one-sided argument I have ever had. For weeks, I had been silently begging my husband to befriend a reporter in order to use his or her satellite phone. I realize this may sound ridiculous. But really! How dare he be concentrating on his job instead of his wife!

With that first hello, however, my irritation turned to uncertainty. I wondered if he was still the same man I fell in love with. Had this experience changed him? Had the past month hardened him? Would details from the home front seem anything but trivial to him now that he had been through a war?

I kept my questions to myself. All I wanted him to know was that I was doing well. The army operates on a need-to-know basis, so I quickly decided that we would, too. As long as he was in the desert, Jay did not need to know that termites have been discovered at our house, or that I had two flat tires in the last month or that the refrigerator broke. He did not need to know that his pay had been incorrect for four months or that I have been scared out of my mind.

For twenty glorious minutes I listened to his stories of Baghdad. He tried to protect my feelings, too, and his tales were not horrific war stories but amazing adventures that he had or sights he has seen. He told me of Saddam's bombed-out palace. We laughed at stories of Udday's palace with lions and wealth galore. He even told me about a single lieutenant he would like to introduce to my sister.

Any awkwardness that I had feared, dissolved. I was overwhelmed with pride; I was so lucky, and my husband was so brave. Military spouses share their lives with fascinating, dedicated individuals. So listening to Jay's firsthand account of the war was truly precious.

The phone line cut out before we were able to say how much we missed each other. I held the phone in my hand for several moments, hoping to hear his voice again. The familiar pain of missing him returned. I waited two months for that wonderful phone call. Now, the waiting starts again.

Jodie Smith

Hello, Beautiful

Taking joy in life is a woman's best cosmetic.

Rosalind Russell

I was at the kitchen table, barely aware of the breakfast waiting in front of me. The untouched eggs were cold. I stared out the window at the dismal December day.

My husband was almost halfway through his third tour in Vietnam, and my near future would include the delivery of our fourth baby and the challenge of caring for an infant while trying to keep up with my other kids. Jimmy, Mike and Tracy were very active children between the ages of six and ten, and it was my job to keep their minds occupied so that the year without their dad would go faster.

I missed my husband, I was tired, and the weight of my bulging belly was pulling on my back. My depression felt justified. The forty extra pounds on my normally thin body made me feel fat and ugly. With my coping skills depleted, I was as low as I had ever let myself get. I just couldn't seem to shake the blues.

My thoughts were interrupted by someone at the front door. After the usual heart pounding that all military wives experience when their husband is in a war zone and the doorbell rings, I opened the door to find a florist standing there with a big box of flowers in his arms.

I thought the delivery was an error since we have no special occasions in December, but my name was on the box. I opened the card and smiled broadly while the pent-up tears streamed down my face. Since that morning, any time I feel sad, I draw on the joy I felt as I stood in the middle of our living room holding those flowers. There were only two words on the card, but they were the ones I most needed: "Hello, beautiful!"

Jane Garvey

Free Mail

The most vital right is the right to love and be loved.

Emma Goldman

I couldn't sleep last night. I lay there in my bed praying to hear from my husband, knowing he couldn't call, but hoping for a letter. It seems like it's been so long since the last one came. I opened my mailbox this morning and there it was—a letter marked "free mail." My heart stopped.

It never ceases to amaze me how much those two little words can mean. Somehow, this letter arrived when I needed it most. I read it right there, standing next to the mailbox. It was written the day before he headed into Iraq from Kuwait, where he had been stationed for the past six weeks. He told me a little bit about what he's been doing, and I tried to picture him in my mind. He shared his feelings about crossing the border, and I could feel those things, too. He told me how much he loved me and the kids, and how our letters were getting him through the days. He said he hoped I hadn't been watching the news, but that he was sure that I had been. He told me he'd been well trained and not to worry about him, then said he knew I would anyway.

Toward the end of the letter, my tears began to fall. Then I read, "Stop crying now, and smile for me." I smiled a big smile and laughed out loud. The next line: "There you go, that's my girl. Your smile makes everything all better." Again, I was reminded of how well he really knew me, and I was comforted, knowing that, even across the miles, he managed to remain so much a part of me. I closed my eyes and imagined him next to me. I remembered the joy of all our reunions from past deployments, and I could feel his arms around me.

Letters can't fix everything, but I treasure them because I understand that "free mail" isn't really free.

Jill Cottrell

How fighter pilots' wives get their husbands' letters.

Mercy

Five o'clock came with the clock every day. The walk came from love.

R. J. Foco

Evangeline was blessed with a loving husband and three gentle children. Her husband Angelito was truly her soul mate and her angel. Angelito enjoyed cooking meals for his young family, playing with his children and helping Evangeline with daily household tasks. He had no aversion to scouring bathrooms, mopping floors, washing dishes or folding laundry. He encouraged his young wife to go out and enjoy her friends while he stayed home looking after the little ones.

Angelito had brought his family to the Hawaiian Islands for a tour of duty in the military service. Evangeline was far from her home in Pampanga, Philippines. She left behind her mother and father to be with her husband. Her husband wrapped her in a blanket of love and her children filled her days. Time went by.

One morning, as Angelito was getting ready to go out for a run, Evangeline noticed a lump on his upper thigh.

She encouraged him to have it examined. It was cancer.

Their sweet life together would now be spent hoping, praying and learning to live with the inevitable. Angelito fought for his life for two years and then quietly lost the battle. Three children were left fatherless: fourteen-year-old B. J., ten-year-old Einar, and little Davin, only two years old. Evangeline lost her partner in life and was left all alone to care for her bereft family.

She was lost on an island, in the middle of the Pacific Ocean, in despair. Evangeline managed to care for the needs of her children, but would collapse in anguish at the end of the day. The most bitter hour for Evangeline was 5:00 P.M.—the big hour. Her husband had always walked in the door at 5:00 P.M., and each day, she couldn't help but wait for him. Of course, he would never come home, and Evangeline would go to bed alone and cry herself to sleep.

Her dear friend recognized this particular agony. And one day, at precisely 5:00 P.M., her friend knocked at the door and insisted Evangeline join her for a walk. After much urging, Evangeline acquiesced. After that, her friend came every day. Sometimes, she would have to come in the house, go into Evangeline's bedroom and insist she get out of bed and walk with her. During these walks, Evangeline would cry and cry. She knew she was free to share her innermost pain and anguish. Her friend just quietly walked beside her, hour after hour, day after day.

They walked in rainstorms. They walked in the summer heat. They walked through the gentle breezes scented with the plumeria blossoms. They walked with the trade winds gusting at their backs. Winter, spring, summer and fall, these two friends walked the road of grief together. This friend walked beside Evangeline for three years! For three years, not a day was missed. Not a day was

Evangeline left alone during "the big hour"; not until her friend sensed that she was strong enough to walk alone.

Mother Teresa remarked: "We can do no great things, only small things with great love." Such a small thing to walk with a friend in her loneliest hour. Such a great love to walk with a friend, day after day, year after year. Such an act of Mercy. And the name of Evangeline's friend? Mercy is her name. Her name is Mercy.

Evangeline Dionisio
As told to Shelly Mecum

Navy Pilot's Wife

*Only when we are no longer afraid do we begin
to live.*

Dorothy Thompson

When you are a navy pilot's wife, every phone call makes
you stiffen, and every knock at the door brings a lump to
your throat and a knot to your stomach. The dangers of
combat are obvious, but even routine flights have inher-
ent dangers. Flying is a perilous business, and families of
pilots face that on a day-to-day basis.

It was a difficult six months when my husband was
deployed as a helicopter pilot in the Persian Gulf region.
We had two daughters, and I was pregnant with our third.
Dennis and I e-mailed each other as much as we could,
trying to support each other from opposite sides of the
world. I faced the challenges of being a temporarily single
parent back home, and he faced the challenges of long, hot
flights over the Persian Gulf.

We talked about everything except the dangers he
faced. He didn't bring it up because he didn't want to
worry me. I didn't bring it up because I didn't want to

burden him with my worries. But the dangers were real, and we both knew it. I knew he was a good pilot, but that didn't stop the nightmares I had of him flying in slow motion, the sand whirling around, the smell of burning fuel and the sound of clicking rotors as his helicopter plummeted to the ground. I never told him about the nightmares, but every time I had them, I awoke shaking and sweaty, with the taste of sand in my mouth.

During spring vacation from school, the girls and I took a trip to South Carolina with my parents. For the first time during Dennis's deployment, I relaxed and let go of the constant worry. He would be home in another month, and all was well. Truthfully, I was relieved to be out of our house, where I had to wonder if every knock on the door might be that of a navy chaplain.

We were walking in from a bike ride when I heard my cell phone ringing. I ran to answer it but could only hear a lot of noise on the other end. "Hello?" I said, then yelled, "HELLO?"

Then, on the other end of the line, I heard, "Sarah? It's me. I'm okay. I need you to know that it wasn't me and that everyone got out okay. I'll call you as soon as I can . . ." and then the phone went dead.

What was he talking about? I had no idea, but I felt my throat tighten and a sandy taste filled my mouth.

"What's wrong, Mom?" my daughter asked.

"I'm not sure, honey," I said, and I walked to the TV and turned it to CNN. The scroll line at the bottom of the screen said: "NAVY HELICOPTER CRASHES."

I got a chill and started to shake. He was okay. I took a deep breath and patted my pregnant belly. "Daddy is okay."

I didn't find out the whole story until later. My husband had been the pilot of one of two helicopters set to fly in formation. He took off first, and, when he turned to spot the other helicopter, he saw it on the ground in flames. Everyone had gotten out of the aircraft, but he didn't know that at the time. He landed nearby and found out that his squadron mates were okay. When he saw a news crew pull up, his first thought was how scared I would be if I saw video of the crashed helicopter on TV. He remembered he had his cell phone in his flight suit pocket, and, just moments after the accident, he called me. Amidst all the chaos, despite how close he and his fellow pilots had come to disaster, he was thinking about protecting me. His selflessness touched me and brought us even closer together.

I haven't dreamed about helicopter crashes since.

Sarah Monagle

The Unseen Veteran

*In order that she may be able to give her hand
with dignity, she must be able to stand alone.*

Margaret Fuller

To understand military life, or what it feels like to be the
proud wife of a soldier, you need to experience it.

One day he was here and now he is gone. . . . He isn't
beside me in bed. . . . His scent slowly fades, as does the
memory of his face. . . . I can barely remember the familiar
sounds of him at home. I long for comfort when I have a
nightmare. I want him to hold me. I wait for those comforting letters or the phone calls that come after three
months of silence.

Now, I look upon single parents in awe . . . and I learn to
do what they do, until my husband comes home. I don't
need a man to put a crib together, to take care of the car or
to take out the trash. I have learned to be empathetic. I
have become self-sufficient.

And even though these are wonderful things, I would
give up everything that I have learned to bring him home
right now.

When I think that I cannot go on, I rely on my routine so that I can support my husband while he defends our freedom. And I know that I am not the only one.

I am an unseen veteran. So are all the other military spouses out there. We have different battlefields. Our maps have pins in the countries of worry, heartache and loneliness. Our battles will end when our husbands are in our arms again. Until that day, I say thank you to all the invisible soldiers who are there for each other, who are there for me. We lend a strong shoulder when needed, and we keep up the brave front at home. The war could not be won without us.

Amanda Legg

3

RAISING MILITARY BRATS

America's future will be determined by the home and the school. The child becomes largely what he is taught; hence, we must watch what we teach, and how we live.

Jane Addams

The Cost of War in Cheerios

Bring such talents as you have, use them, and they will be multiplied.

Ernest Holmes

"Honey, the air campaign started today."

With those few words, countless thoughts exploded in my head. Winds of war already swirled around Fort Campbell. The 101st was poised like a bullet in the barrel, aimed at the heart of the Taliban. When the Department of the Army pulled the trigger, Doug's unit was prepared to be the first shot fired. He was ready. I was ready. But were the children?

Since 9/11, we'd grown uncomfortably familiar with the need to discuss adult realities with our preschoolers. They had seen the towers fall. And, though we were a thousand miles away from New York, the landscape of our neighborhood changed noticeably. Heightened security brought armed guards to every Fort Campbell gate. Armored military vehicles presided over major intersections on the post while aircraft patrolled the skies. And guns, tanks and helicopters soon replaced soccer, ballet and Barney as favorite dinnertime topics.

Douglas drew a deep, solemn breath before he gave voice to our silent conversation. Like other discussions before it, this one brought the dreaded barrage of un-answerable questions: *Do children die in war? Will our daddy have to kill somebody else's daddy? Will our daddy die?* We replied as honestly as we could without adding to their fear and worry. In the end, we focused on the humanitar-ian efforts of our nation toward the Afghan people. We weren't sure what was within their reach, but they under-stood far more than we gave them credit for.

The next morning, Moriah, our four-year-old, scooped dry cereal from her bowl and announced that she needed a Baggie. "Mom," she said seriously, "when Daddy goes to defeat Osama Bin Laden, he can take this to give to the children, so they won't be hungry."

With the same precision that their father uses to pack his rucksack, Moriah and her five-year-old brother Keith carefully filled plastic bags with Cheerios from their own breakfast bowls. That evening, the bags of cereal were cer-emoniously added to the official packing list, poignant reminders of the costs of war and the willingness of little children to pay for it.

Mary C. Chace

"There are no K rations for TLC."

Can't Let Go

War is not nice.

Barbara Bush

I had said good-bye to my husband, Joe, so often, but this time was different.

We now had our first child. After nights of soul-searching and what-ifs, we made the difficult decision that Joe would go by himself to Alabama for the six-month training course, and I would stay behind with our new son. It was important that I hold onto my teaching position near our home at Fort Hood, plus we were part of a strong network of friends whom I could count on to see me through the rough spots.

On Joe's last evening at home—always a melancholy time—I bathed little Joey, got him into his sleeper and was heading to the bedroom when Joe gently touched me on the shoulder. Lifting the baby from my arms, he said he wanted to tuck Joey in tonight.

They headed down the hall, and I busied myself with meaningless tasks, expecting Joe to emerge from the bedroom within a few minutes. A half hour went by, and still he had not come back. Figuring he was having trouble getting our son to fall asleep, I tiptoed to the baby's room and peeked into the dimly lit room.

Sitting in the rocking chair, moving slowly back and forth, was my husband, stifling quiet sobs. He was holding our sleeping infant in his arms as though he would never let go.

I whispered, "Honey, what can I do?"

His pained eyes met mine, and after a moment he mumbled, "I just can't put him down."

That night, we stood over Joey's crib, holding each other, consoling ourselves and saying over and over that we would make it through this separation and be together again soon.

Joey is six now, and he has a four-year-old brother named Jack. There have been many farewells since that night, yet my military hero still fights back tears when it's time to leave once again in service to his country and give his boys that last, long hug good-bye.

Julie Angelo

Strains of Freedom

Life is what happens when you're busy making other plans.

John Lennon

Still groggy from a sleepless night and numb from the previous day's events, I wanted nothing more than to pull him back to bed with me and burrow under the familiar warmth and comfort of our covers, our front door bolted to simulate safety and guard against the terrors of the outside world. Instead, I turned to watch my best friend, my beloved husband of twenty-two years, lace the shoestrings through the eyes of his combat boots. Even in the gray light of dawn, I could clearly see, and shudder at, how different this morning's battle dress uniform was from the customary white-collar attire—air force blues—of his past three-year Pentagon assignment. The change of clothing represented the way that, in less than twenty-four hours, life had changed with such intensity, such ferocity; that for America, "normal" would never be the same.

I followed David down the stairs and to the front door, wrapping my arms around him, burying my face in his chest. I listened for his heartbeat, searching for the scent of his skin beneath the crispness of his freshly starched uniform, losing myself in his embrace. At the same time, I memorized the way he felt within the circle of my arms. I longed to never let go. . . .

Selfishly—for my own comfort. And symbolically—for the ones who would never again hold their loved ones.

Keep him safe, I prayed desperately, struggling to be a good soldier's wife and forcing myself to release him.

I would not cling. That no longer defined our relationship, our actions or us. Despite the fear in my heart, I gave him my bravest smile. "Please God, bring him home to us at the end of this day," I whispered, and he walked to his car and drove away.

Twelve long hours later, he came back to us. Our young son and adolescent daughter raced to meet their daddy at the door, tackling him with their customary hugs and kisses. Our oldest daughter phoned, just to hear his voice.

Still trying to cope with the shock, we forked through our dinner and followed, to the best of our ability, our normal nighttime routine. All the while, we kept an ear to the television to listen for terrorist updates.

The children were sent upstairs to begin getting ready for bed as we turned off the TV, locked the doors and turned out the lights. In the otherwise aircraft-grounded skies, the distant overhead rumble of patrolling jets stopped us at the foot of the stairway. My question spilled out.

"Isn't it hard to go back in there?" I asked. "It's still burning, smoking. It's a graveyard."

"What is hard is that at the end of the day I can come home," David told me.

I nodded, too choked to speak. I thought of the newscast of the woman holding vigil on the hill across the road from the Pentagon, waiting, watching, hoping and praying for any sign, any glimmer, that her loved one might step from the wreckage and rubble. I thought of all the people wandering and searching, and of the posters and flyers emerging in New York City of those lost in the World Trade Center. I clearly understood the meaning of his words.

"God has been good to us," I whispered. "I thought I'd lost you." My tears fell freely. My heart overflowed with thanksgiving, yet at the same time burned with shame, for that very sentence seemed to selfishly invalidate the lives lost. Most assuredly, God loved them and their families, too.

I could tell from his expression that he knew what I was feeling. His eyes were full of his own anger, the pain and demons of needless guilt. And where we could find no words, we reached for each other and held tight, searching for solace, wisdom and a way to understand all that was happening.

It was as we embraced, trying to soothe and fill the emptiness within, that the music began, first as a series of warm-up pizzicato plucks. Soon, the bow met the strings. We smiled at the rusty, scratchy, squeaky notes but then fell somber as the tune from our daughter's violin grew to a recognizable melody. She played on, mellowing into the most lovely, beautiful, childlike rendition of the "Star Spangled Banner" that I have ever been blessed to hear.

Strains of freedom wafted from her bedroom at the end of the hallway, down the stairs to where we stood in the streetlamp-lit foyer. We must have gasped in unison; our hearts jolted, our resolve suddenly growing keen as if we had both taken the first breath after our lungs were punched empty by hatred and bitterness. We pulled apart just enough to look into each other's eyes, where we communicated at a level much deeper than words would have allowed.

"Have I practiced long enough, Mom?" our daughter called from her room.

"Please, just one more time," I called back to her, my voice just a little stronger, a little more sure.

And as she again played the anthem, David and I, hand in hand, began to fill with new hope, resolve and determination. We reached for the banister and stepped onto the bottom step of the flight of stairs. We would climb to hug our children, to love them, to continue our journey as parents. We would teach them love and self-respect, and tolerance and acceptance for our fellow man . . . and tuck them in and kiss them good night.

On that fateful Tuesday of September 11, 2001, the very roots and foundation of America and its citizens were shaken to the core. Yet, one by one, moment by moment, we each found our inspiration to redefine and reestablish the normalcy in our lives, to rise above the atrocities and to find a way to forge ahead in the aftermath. For my husband and me, it was the power of our national anthem, delivered by our daughter's hands, that opened the way to healing.

Tracey L. Sherman

In the Arms of a Soldier

Here I am, where I ought to be.

Louise Erdich

The call came from Barton, my husband. He was asking me to come to Norfolk, Virginia, as soon as possible. "Please bring my little son with you," he pleaded.

His ship had come into port for just a few days, a short stay. Big things were happening in Norfolk, the largest naval base in the United States, with many ships anchored in the area. Barton was sure the war would escalate soon.

I began to pack immediately, to prepare for the journey. Little Michael was just six months old. It would be his first trip. Baby food, diapers and clothing needed to be gathered and packed.

We traveled from my hometown of Ottawa, Ohio, to Cincinnati on the Baltimore and Ohio Railroad. There we transferred to the Norfolk and Western Line, which would take us directly into the large station in Norfolk.

In those days, the railroads were very busy shipping war equipment and transporting the military troops across country to the port cities. The country was at complete mobilization and was at full alert for the active duty of all troops.

Little Michael had six uncles in military service as well as his sailor father.

During the layover in Cincinnati, I was helped by the Travelers Aid Station. They gave me a room where I could feed the baby, heat his bottle and change his diaper. Even a rocking chair was available. We waited there until our train was called.

When we boarded our coach, I found it to be full of military men, mostly sailors. We settled into our seat, and the baby immediately fell asleep. Our journey began, and as we went along, I enjoyed the sight of the beautiful Allegheny Mountains.

When Michael awoke, the sailor sitting next to me asked if he could hold my baby. He held him for a while, and then, when he became more comfortable, he relaxed and even began to speak to the child.

As we journeyed on, the sailor in the seat behind us asked if he could also hold the baby. He was passed over the seat and into the sailor's hands. Across the aisle, another military man asked if he could hold the baby, and so it began.

I was not fearful of the child being passed from one to the other. I could only think that these young men were going to war and there was no certainty as to whether they would return. If that small infant gave them some pleasure, surely they should have it.

They began to pass the baby up and down the coach. They marveled at his tiny hands and fingers, at how he seemed to enjoy the attention with his little smile and content demeanor.

When I seemed to have lost contact with the baby, I walked to the back of the coach and found Michael sound asleep in the arms of a sailor. He asked me to leave the child. "Please don't take him," he said. "Let him sleep, and I'll bring him to you when he awakens." He explained that he had left his little son when he boarded the train in Cincinnati.

As we arrived in the Norfolk station, I just knew that Michael, that tiny child, had given those sailors something special: a reason to serve their country, something to fight for and a determination to return home for better days.

Mary D. Jackson

Hi Daddy

The bitterest tears shed over graves are for words left unsaid and deeds left undone.

Harriet Beecher Stowe

October 29, 2003

Hi Daddy,

Sorry I haven't written to you in a while. A lot of things have been going on. I miss you so much. How have you been? Is heaven everything it says it is? I know it's probably that and more. I can't wait 'till I can come join you again. I miss you so much—just being here for me to hold your hand and you calling me "princess." But one day we can do this again.

But it will be even better because Jesus will be with us. I keep going in your office to see all your things and your awards that you have gotten over the years. You accomplished so much. I am proud you were my daddy; I would not have chosen anyone else. I like to go into your closet, too and just touch and smell all your clothes . . . it gives me so many memories that I miss so much. Sitting at this table I see your writing on a little piece of paper telling me and mom what e-mail and address in Iraq to write to you . . . CSM JAMES D. BLANKENBECLER, 1–44 ADA. I love to just look at your handwriting so much. I have your military ring on right now. It's kind of big for my little finger, but it makes me feel you're holding my hand when I have it on. . . .

It's been on since we found out the news. I have your driver's license with me, too, so I can just look at you whenever I want. You have a little smile this time. When we went to get them done in El Paso I asked you to just smile this time . . . and you did it just for me. I also was looking at your car keys and that little brown leather pouch you always had on your key chain. It made me cry a lot when I picked it up. Everything reminds me of you so much. When we pass by Chili's I remember you sitting across from me eating your favorite salad. You always told the waiter to take off the little white crunchy things . . . because you hated them. And when we drive by billboards that say "An Army of One," it makes me remember you in your military uniform. How you always made a crunching sound when you walked, and how you shined your big boots every night before you went to bed. I miss seeing that all the time. Little things that I took for granted when you were here seem priceless now. One thing that I regret is when you wanted to open my car door for me, but I always got it myself. I wish I would have let you do it. And when you wanted to hold my hand, I sometimes would pull away because I didn't want people to see me holding my daddy's hand . . . I feel so ashamed that I cared what people thought of me walking down the parking lot holding your hand. But now I would give anything just to feel the warmth of your hand holding mine.

I can't believe this has happened to my daddy . . . the best daddy in the whole world. It feels so unreal, like you're still in Iraq. You were only there for 17 days. Why did they have to kill you? Why couldn't they know how loved you are here? Why couldn't they know? You have so many friends that love you with all their hearts and you affected each and every person you have met in your lifetime. Why couldn't they know? When I get shots at the hospital I won't have my daddy's thumb to hold tight. Why couldn't they know I loved for you to call me "princess"? Why couldn't they know if they killed you I would not have a daddy to walk me down the aisle when I get married? Why couldn't they know all this? Why? I know that you are gone now, but it only means that I have another angel watching over me for the rest of my life. That's the only way I can think of this being good. There is no other way I can think of it.

All the kids at my school know about your death. They even had a moment of silence for you at our football game. A lot of my teachers came over to try to comfort me and mom. They all ask if they can get us anything, but the only thing anyone can do is give me my daddy back . . . and I don't think anyone can do that. You always told me and mom you never wanted to die in a stupid way like a car accident or something like that. And you really didn't die in a stupid way . . . you died in the most honorable way a man like you could—protecting me, mom, Joseph, Amanda and the rest of the United States.

In the Bible it says everyone is put on this earth for a purpose, and once they accomplished this you can return to Jesus. I did not know at first what you did so soon to come home to God. But I thought about it—you have done everything. You have been the best husband, father, son and soldier in the world. And everyone knows this.

One of my teachers called me from El Paso and told me that when her dad died, he always told her, "when you walk outside the first star you see is me."

She told me that it is the same for me and you. I needed to talk to you last night, and I walked outside and looked up . . . and I saw the brightest star in the sky. I knew that was you right away, because you are now the brightest star in heaven.

I love you so much, daddy. Only you and I know this. Words can't even begin to show how much. But I tried to tell you in this letter, just a portion of my love for you. I will miss you, daddy, with all of my heart. I will always be your little girl and I will never forget that . . .

I love you daddy, I will miss you!!

P.S. I have never been so proud of my last name.
Sunrise—June 27, 1963
Sunset—October 1, 2003

Jessica Blankenbecler

[EDITORS' NOTE: *Jessica Blankenbecler, fourteen, e-mailed this final letter to her father, Command Sgt. Maj. James Blankenbecler, at 1:29 A.M. on Friday, Oct. 3, 2003, two days after he was killed when his convoy was ambushed in Samarra, Iraq.*]

Doubting Thomas

The best and most beautiful things in the world cannot be seen, nor touched . . . but are felt in the heart.

Helen Keller

"Thomas Tucker rarely stands in front of a crowd," the reporter wrote. This is true. Thomas gets excited around large crowds. When he is overstimulated, he needs an outlet to help calm himself down, like spinning.

My eight-year-old son is autistic. A very polite and loving boy, Thomas is considered "high functioning," which means that he can interact with others. His speech is significantly below age level, and he goes to speech therapy four times a week, but my husband and I try not to treat Thomas like he is different, and we expect him to do and learn things just like any other child. Because of his autism, he can become very focused on a specific subject, and it isn't always easy to get his attention.

We live in a small community in Kentucky, near Fort Campbell. Thomas is very well known here. It seems we cannot go anywhere in town without someone saying "hi"

to him. Usually, I have to remind him to say, "hi," back;
otherwise, he would just walk right by. He has no idea
how popular he is.

My husband had been deployed with the 86th Combat
Support Hospital a month earlier for Operation Iraqi
Freedom, when the Cadiz Renaissance Society planned a
rally to support the troops. They called to see if Thomas
would say the Pledge of Allegiance.

I was concerned about whether or not he would be able
to maintain his focus in front of a large crowd. But he did
know the pledge by heart. And he had been in school for
five years. I knew I was probably more frightened than
my son, so I told the society that Thomas would be glad
to do it.

Decisions like these are usually made in tandem with
my husband, but we hadn't heard from him since his
deployment, and I had no idea when we would get to
speak to each other. Especially since the rally was to support his father and the rest of the troops, I wanted my son
to be able to participate. But what I really wanted, I realized, was for Thomas to tell me what he wanted. Was he
interested in reciting the Pledge of Allegiance at the rally?
And, could he do it?

Thomas doesn't understand war or why Poppa is gone.
The only thing he seems to understand is that Poppa is at
work, although he isn't sure why we took him to work
one day but can't go and pick him up. Showing my feelings around Thomas is difficult because of his limited
comprehension, so my sobbing and sadness are reserved
for the times when he is at school or in bed. And deter-
mining how Thomas feels is near to impossible. So without input from my son or my husband, I agreed that
Thomas would recite the Pledge of Allegiance.

We arrived at the rally a little before 2:00 P.M. It was supposed to be held at the high-school football field, but the

April rains forced us inside the local Baptist church, a building that has large and very beautiful stained-glass windows. When we walked in, all Thomas could see was the windows. He began talking about *The Hunchback of Notre Dame* and was so fixated on the windows that he couldn't answer any of the reporter's questions.

I started to worry. Usually, when Thomas is focused on something, it's very hard to redirect him. Thomas has not been able to participate in the school productions because he wants to make up his own show when he gets to the microphone. Would that happen today?

Our seats were in the front pew of the church, right in front of the stage. There were numerous speakers and presentations, and Thomas enjoyed the music. He seemed to be focusing less on the windows and more on the rally, but I was definitely getting nervous about him being onstage.

The local VFW brought in the colors to post. Then the unthinkable happened. The VFW did not know that Thomas was supposed to say the pledge, and it is usually routine for them to recite it while posting the colors. We followed suit and recited the pledge along with them. When it was over, I was crushed: Thomas thought we were done and it was time to go home. We sat through the rest of the rally, but I'm sure my disappointment was visible to others around me. As the rally concluded, they sent the VFW back in to retire the colors. To our surprise, they asked if Thomas could come up and say the pledge as they took the colors out. This was it!

Thomas and I walked up to the stage. He stepped up to the microphone and spoke confidently and clearly as he recited the Pledge of Allegiance. His words were so precise that I had to take another look to make sure it was really him at the microphone. When he was done, he stepped back and remained still and quiet. I was astounded, and I could feel my eyes beginning to water. My heart swelled with such pride, and I wished my husband had been able to witness this.

My son stood still and quiet as an audience of two hundred people applauded.

I will never doubt Thomas again.

Leah Tucker

My House Is a War Zone

Take your work seriously, but never yourself.

Dame Margot Fonteyn

On any given day, my boys conduct special ops that result in explosions. This is sibling warfare—mostly constitutional skirmishes. I've ruled on issues of privacy: "Yes, you do have to knock before barging into your brother's room to dump cold water on his head." "No, I don't care if that ruins the surprise." Freedom of the press: "You wrote *what* on your brother's notebook?" The right to keep and bear arms: "I understand you need all these rolled-up socks for your munitions supply, but you need to wear socks in the winter. Period."

I've experienced germ warfare: coughing at the table on your neighbor's food, sneezing in your brother's direction or licking all the cookies and then putting them back. I've witnessed psychological warfare, which is all about making someone believe that you've used his toothbrush to swab the toilet.

Being that I am Captain Mom in this little battleship, and admittedly ready for anything, I shouldn't have been a bit surprised when my husband dropped a verbal bombshell into our living room. In ninety-six hours, he'd be in the Middle East war zone. I was hit with a stinging realization: *Aww, crap. I'm married to a navy guy.* It wasn't a real secret or anything, I mean the uniform, dismal pay and horrifyingly long hours were kind of a giveaway. It's just that, during the last year, in the alternate reality that is military family life, I'd come to look upon my future as bordering on idyllic.

In our decade-plus marriage, we've survived deployments (man never home), job combined with war college at night (man home long enough to sleep and shower), overseas tour (man moves us to unrecognizable home) and job combined with master's program (man home for showers, sleeps during class). Clearly, we've done harder stuff for longer periods. The thing is, that was a different guy. The guy they're sending to the Gulf is a man who escaped the Pentagon on 9/11. Since that horrible day, he's read intelligence reports that gave him nightmares, seen photos that made him want to gouge his eyes out, and endured endless limb checks from a nervous son who can't forget where Daddy was that day. The guy who ran home that night was a newly minted dad and husband. One compass point away from death, he became a guy who suddenly wanted to live for more than his job.

The guy they're sending to the desert has spent the last year reading fewer late-night reports and more bedtime stories, less time catching up on e-mail and more time catching fly balls with his sons.

The irony here is that the man loves the sea but hates the sand. He'd rather lick Hampton Boulevard than go to the beach. So, even without the bugs and the bombs, this would be a less-than-ideal situation.

Still, I feel sorriest for our sons. They'll have to come to me with their math homework, so their grades are headed for the toilet. They'd have better luck stopping a dog on the street and having him bark the answer—I'm just that bad. I'll have to assume the driving instruction of our eldest, and I know there's not enough Maalox in the city to help me survive that nerve-racking experience. I'll have to take over tending the yard, which means my annual "death to all growing things" campaign will have to start early this year. Since my husband is leaving in less than a week, I've got a short amount of time to get up to speed on some important issues. I must learn vehicle maintenance, tool identification and the Zen master approach to the breakfast smoothie. Only when we have achieved the proper balance between the banana and the strawberry will the puree be perfect.

Some things just won't get done. Our eldest son must be driven to crew practice at 5:00 A.M. At 5:00 A.M. I'm sleeping like I've been chloroformed. I'm going to have to beg, borrow and bake my way into a good carpool or invest in some smelling salts. I just pray someone else out there is a sucker for brownies.

By the time my husband comes back, I will have written a dozen notes in lip pencil because I can't find a lead version, convinced the kids that Dawn dishwashing soap is perfectly acceptable bubble bath and tricked them into believing that they have to eat their vegetables because right now, Dad's eating dirt.

Hopefully, we'll look back on all this and have a good laugh. Because, after that, I'm going to have a really good cry.

Melissa M. Baumann

"I don't think your father will appreciate
your version of a mess hall."

Baby's First Words

How hard it must be to miss watching your baby grow up. My husband, a navy pilot, deployed when our daughter Claire was just eight months old. She hadn't yet crawled, gotten teeth or said her first word, and he had to get used to hearing stories about all her accomplishments.

I know he was afraid that she would forget him when he was gone, so I made it my personal mission to make sure she remembered him. I showed her pictures every day, set Daddy's face as the screen saver on our computer, even made a doll with Daddy's face on it. I also put together a video of clips of her with her dad. Claire loved to watch that video and would stare at the screen each time I put it on.

About two months after my husband left, he was able to hook up a videophone to a computer and call us. Claire was sitting in my lap when we began our online messenger chat. Suddenly, my husband's picture came up on our screen and we heard his voice saying, "Hi!" Claire climbed from my lap, leaned on the desk and reached up to the computer screen. She put both hands where her dad's face was and said, "Daddy!"

Six thousand miles away, he heard it over the videophone speakers and a huge smile came across his face.

Despite the separation from our baby, she hadn't forgotten him at all. And, thanks to modern technology, he was with us as she spoke her first word.

Sarah Monagle

All in a Day's Duty

The greatest danger to our future is apathy.

Jane Goodall

One afternoon, my son and I sat quietly in the two seats outside the principal's office, waiting our turn to meet with him. My son wasn't in trouble, but my husband and I had concerns that needed to be discussed with the school. The principal, in turn, was waiting for my son's teacher to arrive for our scheduled meeting and had asked us to have a seat in the foyer.

As the noon hour ended, the usual lunchtime bustle surrounded us: parents coming and going, teachers passing through, students running errands for teachers or taking care of business of their own. The secretary answered the constantly ringing telephone, and, as needed, orchestrated the flow of traffic.

During a brief lull in the activity a young boy walked in. His face was flushed and his hair tousled—normal for a little boy coming straight off the playground. By his size and stature, I guessed him to be a first-grader. He timidly approached the secretary's desk.

"What do you need?" the secretary asked.

The young boy answered in such hushed tones that I couldn't hear him.

"The nurse isn't here," the secretary said, "but wait right there and she should be back soon." She motioned for him to stand in the doorway that led to the nurse's office.

The phone rang again, and the secretary turned to answer it. The little boy nodded and did as he was told. When he walked past with downcast eyes, I realized the reason for his office visit. The front of his pants was wet. He'd had an accident and needed a change of clothing.

Quickly, I looked away. I shifted in my seat to try to give the little one some privacy and a sense of dignity in such a humiliating situation. I pulled my son close, hoping he'd never have to endure such an experience.

The bustle around us picked up again as the bell rang, and students and teachers hurried back to class. With each minute that passed, the little boy's head hung lower. Would anyone come to his rescue?

Not the secretary, who sat at her desk sifting through her work, seemingly all but forgetting the little boy.

Not the nurse, who still had not returned to the office.

Not I, who sat just as uncomfortably as the little boy stood, trying to ignore the situation and not appear as if I were staring.

By now, the little boy had begun to cry silently. His shoulders shook and his head hung so low that no one noticed the tears streaming down his cheeks.

No one, that is, except for an airman who stood at the front of the office, waiting, too, for his appointment with the principal. Clad in full battle dress uniform and black combat boots, the airman walked across the room, knelt down and enfolded the sobbing child into his arms.

"It's okay," the airman said. "We'll get you taken care of."

The secretary looked up, saw the embrace and hustled over to the little boy and escorted him into the nurse's office. The airman quietly stepped back and resumed his wait near the front door.

By then, my son's teacher had arrived, and the principal called us into his office. The airman joined us. My son laced his fingers through his daddy's. I squeezed my husband's other hand.

Tracey L. Sherman

War Is Not a Game

All rising to a great place is done by a winding stair.

Sir Francis Bacon

I was eight and my brother, Butch, was eleven when we arrived in Naha, Okinawa, in 1952, after three weeks aboard a government transport ship. We must have driven our mother and the ship's crew crazy with our adventures: playing tag in the engine room and hide-and-seek in the lifeboats. Yet none of those shipboard escapades upset her as much as our visit to the cave. And nothing ever taught me more.

We were elated to join my father, an officer in the U.S. Army already stationed on the island during the Korean War. Uncle Sam provided everything. My mother had a maid, Tamiko, and the schools, post exchange, commissary and hospital were only a short drive away. On weekends, a school bus took us military brats to the movie theater where we saw the latest Flash Gordon serial and a feature film. It was hard to believe we lived on an island in the middle of the Pacific.

Our housing area was new, so much so that the hills surrounding it held a threat. Although eight years had passed since the U.S. invasion of Okinawa, the military hadn't completely cleaned out the caves inside the hills. During World War II, the Japanese hid in those caves. Now, the hills were off limits. Fences bearing warning signs enclosed those deemed most dangerous, but others, like the one behind our house, remained wide open to curious minds.

Mother would wave her hand in that direction. "Don't ever play up there. The hills and caves are dangerous. Your father says you could be killed."

Of course, the warnings only made the adventure seem more inviting. War was still a game to my brother and me. We wanted to be soldiers. Armed with a flashlight, he and I hiked up the hill to see what all the fuss was about.

As we stepped inside one of the caves, dark and dampness enveloped us. Butch turned on the flashlight, and we inched ahead.

Something that resembled a miniature Flash Gordon spaceship lay in a puddle of water. "What's that?" I asked.

"A mortar shell."

I gasped. My knees trembled. "I'm scared. Let's go home before it explodes."

Butch stepped around it. "Don't be chicken. Just stay behind me and walk where I walk. We'll be okay."

Shivering in the cold and rank air, I clasped my shoulders. Water seeped from the gray walls.

"That was a hand grenade," Butch said after stumbling over an object rolling past my feet. He aimed the flashlight. "Don't touch it." It looked like a can of C rations with a pin sticking out of it.

"I wanna go home."

He ignored me, at least for a few more steps. "Look!" he said.

Before us lay a skeleton. I jumped back and leaned against the cave wall. I wanted to run but knew I couldn't, not with all that explosive stuff behind me. "Please, let's go home," I cried.

"Okay, okay," he said with a sense of satisfaction. "Now that we've got a souvenir." He reached down and grabbed the skull.

We climbed out of the cave, and I blinked to adjust my eyes to the blinding sunlight.

Butch said, "Now here's the plan. When we get to the house, I'll go inside alone and see if the coast is clear."

"Uh-uh," I said. Too many times before my brother had left me holding the . . . bag. Yes, that's what we needed, a bag to hide "the souvenir." Then everything would be okay. Pleased with my cleverness, I suggested that.

"Yeah, sure," he said.

As we approached the side of the house, he handed me the skull. "Wait here while I go inside."

Moments later, Butch came out the front door. "Mom and Tamiko are in the kitchen, so I couldn't get the bag, but they're too busy to notice anything. I left the door cracked for you. Hide it on the shelf above our closet."

"But I can't reach that high."

"On tiptoe you can," Butch reassured me.

Skull in hand, I ran up to the front door and crept inside. No one saw me. So far, so good. With the hallway to the bedrooms just around the corner, I tiptoed and turned . . . right into Tamiko! When she saw the body part in my hand, she reeled back and shook with horror, her low moan sharpened into a scream and she ran out the front door, past my laughing brother, never to be seen again.

I didn't think it was funny, because along came Mother. Her puzzled look grew stern when she saw what I carried. She had seen far too much from her army brats to be upset over trifles, but there were limits.

"This time, you've done it," she said with a shake of her head.

Dad and the military police soon arrived, bringing with them swift and severe discipline. Our butts hurt, and, within two days, a fence surrounded the hill. We had broken the rules; we could've been killed. But even before that happened, Mother taught us a more poignant lesson. Sentenced to our room, from the window Butch and I watched her walk up the hill and return the skull to its proper place.

"A brave soldier died there," she told us when she returned. "He fought for his country, and you had no right to disturb his grave. God forbid, someday it may be your turn to fight. War is not a game."

In 1966, I spent the last summer of my youth in France. Orléans was my dad's last duty station; he would retire soon. With college behind me and the real world before me, I stopped at the American cemetery at Colleville-sur-Mer on the way to Orly Airport. Displayed neatly in rows of sorrow were crosses marking the graves of 9,386 of our soldiers who lost their lives in the Normandy invasion. I couldn't swallow the tears. Can we ever forget their sacrifice?

Some may ask why I went to that cemetery. There are more charming places in France for a young man to visit—Paris, the Loire Valley or the Riviera. But I hadn't forgotten what my mother taught me long ago: that war was not a game, that someday I might be called upon to serve. I stepped away and marched to my car with a sense of duty. In the right front seat lay my orders for Vietnam.

Michael J. Jett

Daddy's Angels

Only she who attempts the absurd can achieve the impossible.

Robin Morgan

"Dear Lord, could you please send two angels to protect my daddy? I don't mean to be selfish but, you see, he is six foot five. He may need the wings of both of them to completely cover him. Please let their wings shield him when the guns are fired and the rockets are shot. Let him know that he is protected and give him comfort. Amen."

I asked my girls to pray this prayer every day while my husband was gone, and I repeated a similar prayer many times throughout the day.

Two weeks after my husband's return from Baghdad, he told a story of how he returned to his trailer after midnight and felt that there was an intruder in his small living quarters. When his search revealed nothing, he prepared for bed with a great feeling of peace and comfort. One hour later he was awakened by the sound of rapid gunfire. Lying on his belly with his weapon drawn, he told us how he was never afraid.

My daughter asked him how this was possible.

My husband told her that he could feel someone in the room protecting him. Actually, he said, it felt more like two. My daughter's eyes grew wide as she looked at me and said quietly, "Daddy's angels."

This was the first my husband had heard of our special prayer for him.

Tammy Ross

You Are on Speaker Phone

Your dreams can come true if you know what to do.

Johnnie Coleman

I think every military wife will tell you that one of the hardest things is being a "Daddy substitute" when Daddy is gone.

In our house, my husband's special time with our three-year-old is bath time. For thirty minutes a day, one on one, they sing "Old MacDonald" at the top of their lungs, practice the ABCs and discuss their days between laughs and splashes. Next, Braeden runs down the hall to his bedroom with Daddy close behind, puts on his favorite Superman pajamas and carefully adjusts his cape. After "flying" through the house to clean up the toys, my husband calls out, "Time to pick out a book."

These moments are my favorite.

We settle together on Braeden's bed and read a carefully chosen story: me, my husband, our son and our newborn daughter. We pray as a family, thanking God for one another, and, of course, for baseball and football! As we say good night, we sing his favorite song, "The Great Big Book of Everything," kiss all three of his stuffed animals, cover him with his two favorite "blankies" and begin the debate of who loves whom more. That is when we receive our reward, and our precious little boy says the magic words. "I love you, Mom and Dad."

When Daddy leaves, the bedtime routine is suddenly turned upside down. Our "key player" is absent from the game. Thanks to modern technology, we have a fix for it. While Braeden is in the tub, we talk about what Daddy is doing. Pj's go on, toys are picked up and then I say, "You pick out a book, and I'll call Daddy."

We all get into bed together: me, our son, our daughter and the telephone.

"You are on speaker phone," I tell my husband. I read the story, and we pray as a family, thanking God for each other, for the day and for Daddy's safe and speedy return. We sing the beloved Disney song, I do all the kisses and then we debate over who loves whom more. Before we end the call, my husband yells out, "I love you, bud." And we are rewarded with our son's reply.

"I love you, Mom and Dad."

Angela Keane

4

HOLIDAYS—
MILITARY
STYLE

God's gifts put man's best dreams to shame.

Elizabeth Barrett Browning

Red, White and Blue Christmas

Honey, you're gone, you're so far away!
And you know that I miss you each and every day!
Things are so much harder this special time of year.
Because you are my gift, and I wish you were here.
Now don't get me wrong, I'm so very proud,
And I'll be the first to say it out loud.
Although I am lonely, I'll get through each night,
Knowing you're out there to fight for what's right.
Baby, I love you and think you're so brave,
And this Christmas I thank you that my flag proudly waves!

Roxanne Chase

Our Matchbox Christmas

Sharing is sometimes more demanding than giving.

Mary Catherine Bateson

It was a rainy California Christmas Eve. Our tree was lit up, and it shone through the large picture window of our home in military quarters at Port Hueneme. My husband would finally be spending Christmas with us. He had often missed the holidays due to deployments, leaving me and our three small children alone for Christmas. He had just returned home from Vietnam and would be home for six months. Then he would have to go back to fighting the war in Vietnam.

Our children, six, four and two years old, were anxiously waiting for their daddy to return from battalion headquarters. He had to "muster and make it." Their little noses had been pressed against the big frosty window almost all afternoon, waiting for him to come back home.

Their daddy was a Seabee, and we were all as proud of him as we could be, but we often struggled to make ends meet. Once a month, I would buy a month's worth of groceries, and this month, I had managed to squeeze in a large turkey and all the trimmings, to cook for our Christmas Eve meal, but money for presents was scarce. I had bought my husband a small gift, and he had bought me one. The children each had a handful of tiny department-store toys, all individually wrapped and waiting for the big day. There were no names on the small gifts; I could feel through the paper and tell what they were.

I saw my husband's car headlights cut through the dark winter mist that engulfed our home. I pushed back my hair and straightened my clothes. The children and I rushed to the door. This was our big night! It had been our tradition back home in Texas to eat our big meal on Christmas Eve night, and this year we were going to eat better than we usually did. Our little table was laden with all sorts of tasty-looking food. Each of the kids would get to open one present, and Santa Claus would be coming after they went to sleep.

To my surprise, when I opened the door to give my husband a big kiss, standing behind him were three burly Seabees. They hung their heads as they entered our home, as if to apologize for intruding on our family feast.

"Honey," my husband said, almost apologetically, "these are some of the guys who were with me in 'Nam. Their families are thousands of miles away. They were just sitting in the barracks, and I asked them if they wanted to come eat with us. Is it okay if they stay?"

I was thrilled to have Christmas company. We, too, were thousands of miles away from friends and family. It had been so long since we had "entertained." We gladly shared our small feast with those three huge Seabees. After dinner, we all sat down in the living room. The children started begging to open their gifts. I sat them down and walked over to the tree to get them each a tiny wrapped gift.

As I glanced up, I could see my husband's friends sitting there looking sad and distant. I realized how bittersweet it must feel to be here with us. I knew they must be thinking about their own children, wives and homes. They were staring down at the floor, lost in the loneliness of the season, trying to shake the horrible memories of the war they had just left—a war to which they would soon return.

Quickly, I scooped up six colorfully wrapped Matchbox cars. I called each of our children's names, and they quickly opened their presents. Soon, all three of them were rolling their cars on the floor.

I walked over to the men. "Well, what do you know?" I said. "Old Santa must have known you were going to be here!"

Those big old Seabees looked up in surprise. They opened their treasures: a Matchbox car for each of them. Within seconds after they opened the gifts, those men were grinning from ear to ear, down on the floor playing with their tiny cars.

I looked up at my husband. "How about me?" he asked. "Did Santa leave me anything?"

I reached under the tree and handed him a tiny present also. He joyfully joined our children and his friends. They must have played for hours. They ate, told funny stories and laughed while they rolled those race cars around on the floor.

I watched them there, filled with pride. These men had fought for us and kept us free. Free to have nights like this one, and others that were to come.

I didn't really know these men, but there they were, sitting on our floor. They would have given the world to be back home with their loved ones, but it wasn't possible. They had committed to defend our country. They were trying to make the best of an awful time in their lives.

Soon, the races were over, the food was almost all devoured, and each of the men said their good-byes and left our home, their faces shining with new hope. In each of their hands, clutched tightly, was a tiny Matchbox car.

Years have passed since that Christmas Eve night. Two of the men returned from the war. One didn't.

We have seen them over the years, visited their homes, met their families. The men have swapped war stories while the women shared "left at home to do it all by ourselves" stories. Our children played together.

When we first met again, I was surprised to learn that every one of the men had kept their cars in their pockets when they were in 'Nam. When times got tough, and everything would get still, the men would quietly take out those little cars. They would give each other a grin, as if to promise that there would be another race and that they would see another day.

And they showed me how, high on a mantel, or proudly displayed in a shadow box, safely tucked away from harm, they still have their tiny Matchbox cars!

Alice Smith

"When I said we needed a more
durable vehicle, I meant . . ."

Spouse of a Soldier

*He has not learned the lesson of life who does
not every day surmount a fear.*

Ralph Waldo Emerson

It was 1990. The winds of war were swirling fiercely. My
husband was an F-16 pilot, and I knew he would be leaving soon. I had received many words of support and comfort from friends and family, for which I was very grateful.
Still, terror gripped me.

I knelt in church on Thanksgiving Day and felt the
warm stream of tears flow. A small age-worn hand
grasped mine. The tiny, frail woman next to me understood: she had sent her husband to World War II, her son
to Vietnam and now her grandson, my husband, to Desert
Shield. From this diminutive form, I drew great strength.
For the sake of my husband, my children and my country, I could now hold back the tears.

Not long after the New Year dawned, my husband and
his comrades strapped into their jets and headed over
the ocean. We wives banded together. We laughed
together and cried together. We commiserated over all

the household catastrophes that only happen when husbands are away. We didn't speak too much about our fears; those were understood.

Inside I quaked with every Scud launch. Every report of a downed plane wrenched my soul. Yet, before anyone else could see the strain on my face, one of the wives would see it. She understood. She would speak no words, but would grasp my hands. I would do the same for her.

The day came when our husbands returned. I had heard that they were coming but was afraid to get my hopes up. Part of me was steeled for my husband to be missing. When I saw him step into the hangar, tired and worn, I felt like a new bride.

After the band stopped playing, the parade was over, the hugs and kisses were given and he was home, I could only cry and tremble the way you do after a near-miss, head-on collision. I thanked God for my husband's safe return. I thanked God for the loving support of family and friends. I thanked God for the strength of the wives. He understood.

Ten years later, we are called spouses, not wives. The last decade has wrought many changes. Some things, however, remain constant. Whether husband or wife, we are still married to soldiers. When duty calls, the soldier will answer. In fact, he may seem eager to leave those he loves and fight the good fight. It is hard to be married to a hero.

A soldier is called to fight, and the spouse of a soldier is called to understand. Understanding makes you a hero, too.

Denise J. Hunnell

Angels Shop at Wal-Mart

No one has ever become poor by giving.

Anne Frank

It was November in San Diego, and with Christmas on the way, many people were out doing their normal holiday shopping. My two daughters and I were shopping for something very different. My husband, an officer in the U.S. Navy, was due to return home from a six-month deployment in the Middle East. This had been my first deployment as his wife, and it had been a tremendous experience. From a broken-down van, to crazy neighbors, to family drama and even a major illness . . . we had overcome it all!

The ship would be pulling in soon, and I had so many wonderful things planned for his homecoming. I had redone the house, let my hair grow and prepared various other "major" surprises. I hadn't seen my husband in almost six months, and I had to look my best. So off we went to Wal-Mart, where I told everyone within earshot that my husband was coming home from deployment and I had to look perfect. See, being a proud navy wife, you tend to get *overly* excited when it comes to homecomings.

We looked through the clothes racks and found outfits for the girls. They looked like models! I was another story. I tried on piles of clothing, asking strangers and salespeople for their opinions. No matter how positive the verdicts, I still wasn't sure.

As my daughters delivered their usual "you never buy yourself anything" routine, I looked down at the tags and gasped. There was no way I could afford this, so I led my daughters out of the store, explaining our financial limitations as we left. I decided that I would find something in my own closet rather than paying sixty dollars for something new. After all, he wasn't coming home to see my new clothes—he wanted to see *me*!

As we wandered out, a woman walked up to me and handed me a piece of paper. I was dumbfounded and, I will admit, a bit nervous. She practically ran away from us. I looked down and opened the yellow paper. It was a note thanking my husband and me, and blessing us both. Included were three twenty-dollar bills. I was terribly confused, and although we searched for the lady all over the store, she was nowhere to be found.

My oldest daughter turned to me and said, "Mom, you know what this means, don't you?"

I was puzzled.

"Now you have to turn it around and bless someone else." How many eleven-year-olds can think so passionately? I couldn't have been more proud of her at that moment.

The woman was nowhere to be found, but I couldn't leave without trying, so I asked an employee if I could use the PA system to deliver a message. He asked his supervisor, and they agreed to let me. My message was this: "To the angel shopping in Wal-Mart, this navy wife would like to thank you and say God bless you."

Jilleen Kesler

A Military Family

Love bears all things, hopes all things, endures all things.

1 Corinthians 13:7

Today marks six months that my son's daddy has been deployed to Southwest Asia. He's fighting to free the people of Iraq. He telephoned last night to tell his five-year-old son, "Happy Easter." He was sorry that he couldn't send some special holiday goodies but knew we'd understand. After all, he'd missed Halloween, Thanksgiving and Christmas. My father passed away, and my husband was able to come home for a few days to attend the funeral. He left again on Valentine's Day. Easter was just another day for me without the man I love. But this was easier for me: I've spent most of my life in a uniform that matches his.

We met during Desert Shield, and have been through several deployments and many "TDY" trips apart from each other. I am used to separation. It is part of being a soldier. We joined to serve our country and have given a combined fifty years of service to a land in which the passing flag still brings a tear to our eyes.

Our little boy was brought into the world at Fort Bragg, the land of "Hooah," airborne soldiers. His first memories are of Daddy jumping out of airplanes. At five, he has already lived in three different duty stations and spent countless hours in daycare facilities. He has become an intelligent youngster with a keen sense of current affairs, and he can point out most countries on the map of the world and tell you about the people who live there. He understands what soldiers do because most of the adults he knows either wear a uniform or are married to someone who does. It is because of him that I watch the news again! We have open discussions about what we hear, and he challenges my opinions. We learn about the world together.

My husband told me last night that we would soon have to make the important decision of whether to stay in and try for general officer, or retire from the military for good. He implied that it would be a family decision, so I asked our son for his input. I tried to explain our options to this small version of his father. I was sure he would say how much he missed his daddy and how much he wants him to come home. After all, he tells me that every day.

He said, "My daddy is a great leader. He'd look good with a star."

As I dropped him off at preschool, I thought to myself how grown up he was, this little soldier of ours. He is the bravest, most dedicated one of all. It is he who has made the greatest sacrifice so his daddy can protect others.

Terry Hurley

·

A Simple Act of Kindness

Love and do as you please.

St. Augustine

Valentine's Day, 2003. I went out to dinner with my mother and my two daughters, three-year-old Hannah and Baby Hope. Kevin, my husband, was working in Charleston, and my dad was out of town. We chose one of our favorite Chinese restaurants, an interesting sight for the other diners: four girls out for a Valentine's dinner!

We had a nice evening. My daughters and I had just arrived in Waterloo the night before, so my mom and I spent the meal catching up on my life. She asked me about Kevin's deployment and how he liked his new squadron. I answered her questions and told her about a friend of ours who was going to be deployed for quite a length of time. Then we moved on to other topics.

When it came time to pay the bill, our waitress came to the table and told us that it had already been taken care of. A man sitting near us had paid for our meal! We looked at him, confused. Our benefactor was embarrassed that the waitress told us who had paid for the meal, as he had intended for it to be anonymous. He looked at me and said, "I overheard you say that your husband was in the military." I was touched by his statement as well as a bit flustered. It is not often that someone stops to say thank you for all the work my husband does to defend this nation, and for the sacrifices we make as a military family.

Before we left, I went up to his table to thank him once more. It was so nice to feel special, especially on Valentine's Day when our family members were miles away. He explained that he comes to that restaurant often, and occasionally looks for someone to treat to dinner. His simple speech brought tears to my eyes.

"Thank you for all that you do," he said, "and please thank your husband for defending our country."

Jennifer Minor

An Extra Chair

Faced with a crisis, the man of character falls back on himself.

Charles de Gaulle

Everyone in the military knows about missing family at holiday times. It's just too far to travel, we explain to the folks back home. With no time for a pass or too little leave time left, we find ourselves celebrating surrounded by neighbors instead of cousins. In fact, I've been away from family during holidays in my married life more than I've been with them.

The first time it happened, it left me feeling quite sad. But it wasn't long before my sadness was replaced with . . . panic. "Wait a minute," I cried. "If we're not going home, then who is going to cook the turkey dinner?"

"You can do it," my dear husband replied. "You'll do a great job. And, by the way, I invited that nice lieutenant with the wife and baby to join us."

At this point, I got on the phone and begged my mom and grandmother for as much advice as they could give. "Plan on a half-pound of meat per person," they said. "Don't forget the hard-boiled eggs in the gravy. Never, ever used canned sweet potatoes. And make sure you have a lovely centerpiece."

Twenty-four hours and three cookbooks later, I had Thanksgiving dinner on the table. There was a small disaster involving a mixing bowl dropped in the middle of an uncooked pumpkin pie. (Friendly advice: Remove pumpkin from the ceiling before it dries.) But Grandmother's candied yams made the house smell just like home, and my first turkey wasn't too bad. It seemed like I had just gotten the kitchen clean, though, when it was time to do it all over again for Christmas.

The next several holidays found us far from home, and the crowd around our table continued to grow. We quickly discovered the only thing worse than being a married couple far from home is being a single soldier. So we invested in some more folding chairs and invited as many as we could.

Once I figured out how long it actually takes to thaw a turkey and how to get the cranberry sauce out of the can, I began to enjoy preparing big meals for crowds. Soon, we began to invite the new members of the unit over for a welcome meal when they arrived. Though I forsook the turkey dinner for something easier, like chicken enchiladas, it became a sort of family tradition for us.

Over the years, we have fed old friends, brand-new acquaintances, foreign visitors and surprise guests. I've learned the wisdom of having a big bag of frozen pasta always available, just in case a crowd gathers. And I have not ended a single one of those dinner parties with regret.

Recently, we've been stationed much closer to home, and I haven't cooked a turkey in a couple of years. I am delighted to step down and let the experts do the preparing, and thrilled to be sitting next to my cousins again. But I wonder about those left behind at the post. I hope someone there has thawed an extra-big turkey, and remembered to get more folding chairs.

Susanna H. Bartee

Christmas—
Military-Family Style

*We are not what we know but what we are
willing to learn.*

Mary Catherine Bateson

I was a child of the Great Depression and all its depriva-
tion. World War II soon followed, which brought rationing.
Food was rationed, especially sweets and sugars, fats and
oils. Red meat was nonexistent, although fish and fowl
were occasionally available. Shoes were rationed (two
pairs per year), as was gasoline. Many "luxury" items were
scarce. Car manufacturing had ceased.

In 1944, my husband was stationed at Peterson Field,
Colorado, as a four-engine plane instructor. Each day, he
walked through the commissary and PX, looking for Chux
(the first disposable diapers), baby furniture or anything
that we might use for our crawling ten-month-old. On one
of these forays, just before Christmas, he bought a twenty-
three-pound frozen turkey and a white enamel combinet
(diaper pail) with a lid, to be used later when the baby out-
grew the disposables.

Just as my husband hunted for bargains, I economized with food, and everything else, by following the admonition of the ladies' society at church: Use it up, wear it out; make it do, or do without. I knew that everyone was experiencing similar circumstances, but that didn't calm my panic. My mother-in-law was coming for Christmas dinner, and to see her first and only grandchild. I had only seen my husband's immediate family three times since our wedding. Now, twenty months and seven moves into our marriage, his mother, father and younger brother were coming for Christmas—and would be sampling my cooking!

The only winterized summer cabin at Green Mountain Falls served as our living quarters. From our front picture window, we could see the twin-engine mail plane flying against the incredibly beautiful winter snow and icescape each morning and night. But I had to forget the beauty for the moment and focus on Christmas dinner!

Our cabin had a coal furnace in the basement, a huge six-burner coal stove in the kitchen and a two-burner kerosene burner, which is what I used to heat water and for the small amount of cooking I did. There were several small saucepans and a teakettle—no large pots or kettles. No roasting pan. No dishes.

My husband found several things at the post stores. He bought sturdy paper plates and cups. We had eight place settings of sterling flatware, plus a few serving spoons. There were a few pieces of my early American crystal still intact after all the moves that could possibly be used for service vehicles—a punch bowl, a smaller bowl, a few salad plates.

The family arrived on Christmas Eve. We drove down to the Antlers Hotel and ate lunch there. We went sightseeing at the Garden of the Gods. We visited the new Broadmoor Hotel ice-skating arena, and treated our guests to an evening meal there.

Back at the cabin, I went to sleep still nervous and wondering how on earth I would feed them the next day. I would learn quickly.

The next morning, while I was still bathing and dressing the baby, my mother-in-law spied the as-yet-unused combinet and latched on to it, hauling it off to the kitchen, where she ordered Dad to fire up the monstrous coal range. Mom scalded the pail and its lid at least six times. She disjointed the turkey and managed to fit it all in, along with salt, pepper, onion, basil, sage, poultry seasoning and goodness knows what else—anything she could find. Soon our cabin had the most delightful aroma of Christmas dinner. She made use of the cabin's percolator by adding cinnamon and other spices to mull some apple cider. Grinning, Dad kept reminding us frequently to "Keep close check on that slop jar; that slop smells good and I would hate for it to scorch." We sat down to what seemed like the most delicious of feasts.

What a great lesson in improvising and making do I learned from my mother-in-law, not only on Christmas day but throughout that wonderful weeklong visit. Dad taught me the value of pleasantness and humor throughout a testy situation. That will always be my most memorable Christmas, when far from home, we turned war and rationing into a holiday of food, fun and family unity.

Marjorie H. Lewis

The 25 Days of Christmas

She was an artist of the ordinary. . . . She painted with the colors of her heart.

Kent Nerburn

Christmas. A treasured family holiday, a time full of joy and love—and my husband Shawn was six thousand miles from home in Iraq. I felt no joy, and my heart ached for him. How could Christmas feel like Christmas this year? This would be the first Christmas we would spend apart in our six years of marriage. And something greater pulled at my heart. Our daughter Faith, six months old and born while Daddy was in Iraq, would have her first Christmas with Mommy . . . but no Daddy. My heart hurt, and my mood was gloomy.

I knew I had to quit focusing on what I couldn't change. If not for my sake, for Faith's. My heartache was killing the holiday, and I didn't want that for any of us. I decided that a person can either have a pity-party or pick herself up and make the best of it.

I began racking my brain. How could I find joy in such an unhappy situation? How would I help it be Christmas for us? I knew it would be especially difficult for Shawn to get in the mood, being in a desert with no good-old North Dakota snow or traditional mistletoe. And, then, it hit me: Why couldn't he have snow, or, at least, the mistletoe, over there?

I decided to send him a care package labeled, "The 25 days of Christmas." There would be twenty-five gifts, each a reminder of our treasured holiday. However, there was a rule for the package: He could only open one gift each day until Christmas. That would be tough for him, I knew, but it would give him something to look forward to every day. Besides, isn't torturous anticipation of opening gifts part of Christmas? That thought put a loving smirk on my face!

My excitement built as I began putting together his package full of Christmas touches: a pine-tree–scented air-freshener so he could have the smell of Christmas, a candy cane so he could have the taste of Christmas, a Christmas music CD so he could have the sounds of Christmas, some cotton balls so he could have some snow for Christmas, hot cocoa so he could have a sip of Christmas. . . . Well, maybe he'd have to make it chilled cocoa! And, of course, the mistletoe, with instructions pending his arrival home.

Putting together this package put the spirit of Christmas in my heart. When Shawn finally received the package and called to thank me, I could hear it in his voice, too. And I guess you could say Christmas for us was what it was supposed to be—full of joy and full of love.

I mentioned the rule that he could only open one gift at a time each day until Christmas. . . . Well, this year for Shawn we'll have to mark "naughty" instead of "nice" for when Santa's "making his list and checking it twice."

Chanda Stelter

READER/CUSTOMER CARE SURVEY

We care about your opinions! Please take a moment to fill out our online Reader Survey at **http://survey.hcibooks.com**. As a **"THANK YOU"** you will receive a **VALUABLE INSTANT COUPON** towards future book purchases as well as a **SPECIAL GIFT** available only online! Or, you may mail this card back to us and we will send you a copy of our exciting catalog with your valuable coupon inside.

(PLEASE PRINT IN ALL CAPS)

First Name _____ MI. ___ Last Name _____

Address _____ City _____

State ___ Zip _____ Email _____

1. Gender
- ❑ Female ❑ Male

2. Age
- ❑ 8 or younger
- ❑ 9-12   ❑ 13-16
- ❑ 17-20   ❑ 21-30
- ❑ 31+

3. Did you receive this book as a gift?
- ❑ Yes   ❑ No

4. Annual Household Income
- ❑ under $25,000
- ❑ $25,000 - $34,999
- ❑ $35,000 - $49,999
- ❑ $50,000 - $74,999
- ❑ over $75,000

5. What are the ages of the children living in your house?
- ❑ 0 - 14   ❑ 15+

6. Marital Status
- ❑ Single
- ❑ Married
- ❑ Divorced
- ❑ Widowed

7. How did you find out about the book?
(please choose one)
- ❑ Recommendation
- ❑ Store Display
- ❑ Online
- ❑ Catalog/Mailing
- ❑ Interview/Review

8. Where do you usually buy books?
(please choose one)
- ❑ Bookstore
- ❑ Online
- ❑ Book Club/Mail Order
- ❑ Price Club (Sam's Club, Costco's, etc.)
- ❑ Retail Store (Target, Wal-Mart, etc.)

9. What subject do you enjoy reading about the most?
(please choose one)
- ❑ Parenting/Family
- ❑ Relationships
- ❑ Recovery/Addictions
- ❑ Health/Nutrition
- ❑ Christianity
- ❑ Spirituality/Inspiration
- ❑ Business Self-help
- ❑ Women's Issues
- ❑ Sports

10. What attracts you most to a book?
(please choose one)
- ❑ Title
- ❑ Cover Design
- ❑ Author
- ❑ Content

TAPE IN MIDDLE; DO NOT STAPLE

BUSINESS REPLY MAIL

FIRST-CLASS MAIL   PERMIT NO 45   DEERFIELD BEACH, FL

POSTAGE WILL BE PAID BY ADDRESSEE

Chicken Soup for the Soul®
3201 SW 15th Street
Deerfield Beach FL 33442-9875

|ııllıııllıılıılılıılıılıllllıılıılıılıılıılılıllıl

FOLD HERE

Do you have your own Chicken Soup story
that you would like to send us?
Please submit at: **www.chickensoup.com**

Comments

5

HONEY, WE'VE GOT ORDERS

My address is like my shoes. It travels with me.

Mother Mary Jones

Keep the House

Life isn't one straight line. Most of us have to be transplanted, like a tree, before we blossom.

Louise Nevelson

My husband and I met in the army. We fell in love and got married at the nearest justice of the peace before our separate, conflicting orders put us on opposite ends of the globe. Soon, I became pregnant and left active duty, the toughest job I had known. We moved to Germany, and had two children. Gradually, my status as a stay-at-home mom made me the most important person in the world to those little people. Instead of missing the active army, I shuddered at the thought of going back.

When 9/11 happened, I was pregnant with our third child. A few months later, we were in the middle of another move. The kids and I stayed with my parents over the holidays, and my husband went on to Fort Drum, New York, and found us a place to live. I was thrilled. It was going to be the longest we had been in one place—maybe a whole three years! I eagerly started planning.

A week later, he called me. "You'd better sit down," he

said. "I'm being deployed. I don't know where, and I don't know for how long. But I leave in two days. Do you want to keep the house?"

We had been through deployments before, and yet I cried and cried, unable to hold it in. We had been about to get our lives together, and we had just found a new house. I considered my options. The kids weren't in school yet; I could stay with my parents and have the baby in Colorado. *At least I would have help,* I told myself. If I did make the move to New York, I'd be forced to rely on strangers—my worst nightmare. But, still, I wanted to have a place that was ours, and a place he could come home to.

I thought about it all night and called him back the next day. "Keep the house," I said.

By mid-December, I was seven months pregnant, and it had been ages since I heard from him. Each day, I waddled out to the mailbox at my parents' house, hoping for a letter, something. One day, I pulled out a manila envelope from the Department of the Army with orders calling me back to active duty. My pregnancy exempted me, but it made me think about what my life would be like if I had to endure six months to a year without my children. Yet, my husband did it all the time. I decided that life waits for no one, and gathered my resolve to make the most of moving.

Shortly after Christmas, I packed up our van and embarked on a three-day journey to New York with two toddlers and a small dog that whines on road trips. Family and friends put us up along the way, and we reached Fort Drum on New Year's Eve, just after a huge snowstorm. I dug out our new address and pulled up next to where the sidewalk should have been. I was looking at three feet of snow. Not only was getting in the driveway impossible, but I didn't own any boots.

I searched the stark landscape and saw a man down the street with a snow blower. I waddled down the street toward him and introduced myself. I asked to borrow his machine to get into my driveway. Instead, he came and did it for me. I was exhausted, but I showed the kids around our dark, cold and empty house. Our furniture was on its way, but I was too pregnant to even dream of moving furniture and lifting boxes. Disheartened and lonely, I sat down and cried. I was used to being self-reliant, but I realized this was going to be a tough winter.

Over the next few weeks, however, I met some incredible people. I had neighbors who brought cookies and shoveled snow. Strangers called me up out of the blue to ask if I needed help moving things. Guys from my husband's unit—who hadn't even met him yet—showed up well after duty hours to move furniture around and help me get set up. Other wives offered to take the kids for a while.

A few months later, my mom flew out to take my husband's place at my side, and I had our baby surrounded by the support and love of the strangers I now called friends. Ladies brought food and gifts to my door for days afterward, and I was overwhelmed by their generosity. I cried a big thank-you to God for surrounding me with so many wonderful friends and family. I cried in relief that I had succeeded, and for the strength of other military wives who give so much to help those who need it so desperately.

Today, I am giving back by helping new wives in our community "keep the house." No one can do it alone, and when you are in a community of army wives, you don't have to.

Jennifer Oscar

Honorable Gift

Love is a choice you make from moment to moment.

Barbara De Angelis

"Mama-San, stop working on your lists. I bring you a cup of coffee. The obi screen is finished so I have story to tell," Mura-San, our Japanese maid, said.

We only had six weeks left in Japan. Time to clean out, pack up, rush to see all we'd missed and begin to say our good-byes. Terry's three-year tour at the Naval Hospital, Yokosuka, had flown by. In June 1972, we would leave for San Diego and his retirement from the navy.

Three years ago, I was warned, "Don't buy anything the first year. Take time to learn what you really like."

I found I loved the fabrics used to create kimonos and their wide sashes called obis. Old fabric was a treasure, since, being flammable, most did not survive World War II. I told Mura-San to let me know if she ever heard of any antique obis for sale.

Weeks later she brought me a tissue-wrapped bundle. It contained a lovely cream, peach and pale-green floral obi.

I loved it. "What do I owe you for the obi?" I asked.

"I give to you. A friend owe me a favor. She gave me her obi. You will have a screen made from it to honor the obi," Mura-San said.

I was busy attending a university, with three teenage children, a husband and military social obligations. I put the obi in the rosewood chest and procrastinated. One day, exasperated by my dawdling, Mura-San announced that we were taking the obi to Yokohama's Motomachi Street to visit the screen maker's shop.

The screen maker didn't speak English, and my Japanese was barely basic, so Mura-San haggled, explained, discussed dimensions and timing. It would cost about seventy-two thousand yen (three hundred dollars) and would be ready in a month.

Now, on this May day, the screen stood, in the corner of the dining room, wrapped and packed for shipping.

I sipped my coffee and watched Mura-San glide gracefully as she carried her cup and a box of tissues to the table. Japanese women her age, trained in childhood to walk in wooden *geta*, walked like swans skimming a pond. She was short, solid with middle age and wore her gray-streaked black hair in a simple pageboy cut. She could read and write English as well as speak it. I knew very little of her life; she had never married and she lived alone in a small house on a narrow, winding lane near downtown Yokohama.

We often sat together discussing menus, shopping lists and the children's schedules. She knew the details of our daily lives while I knew little of hers. I depended on her to help my husband and me keep our lives running smoothly. I could not have attended Sophia University in Tokyo, two nights a week, without her help at home.

She wiped her eyes, sipped the coffee she loved, took a deep breath, and began: "I was sixteen years old and still in school when my father decided it was time to arrange a marriage for me. He chose a twenty-year-old man named Yoshi. Our families were friends. My father would not have forced me into marriage, but I liked Yoshi. Girls were expected to marry and have grandchildren for their parents. We were taught that love and devotion came after marriage.

"Yoshi and I became engaged, which pleased both families. My mother and aunts spent much time shopping for new clothes for me to wear to all the parties and dinners planned for Yoshi and me. We made many trips to kimono makers and obi shops. There were elegant silks for dress up and cottons for everyday. We wore kimono whenever we went out. My favorite outfit was the one I wore to the formal engagement party. It was in mid-August 1941. I was very hot in those layers of clothing, and I was so nervous I perspired. I was afraid I would ruin my new kimono and obi. The wedding was planned for the next spring at cherry-blossom time.

"Yoshi was called to join the air force in February of 1942. When I told him good-bye, I knew he might not return."

Tears welled in her eyes and her hand trembled as she took a sip from her cup. "Maybe you would like to tell me the rest later," I said.

"No, I have to tell it all now," she replied. "When the bombing planes started coming over Japan, my father decided to move to an old farm in the country that had been his parents' home. He told each of us that we could bury some treasured things in a cave at the bottom of the bluffs of our property. I chose my favorite obi. It was woven in Kyoto and was cream color with coral and green. It had some sweat stains and a small tear, but it reminded me of Yoshi. I rolled the obi and squeezed it into a large glass jar with a screw-on top. In the night, as the bombers roared overhead, Father and my two elder brothers took our treasures to the cave. They rolled rocks and dirt over the opening.

"We lived on the farm for two years. When the war ended, we returned to Yokohama. One of my brothers was killed on Okinawa. Yoshi's plane went down during a sea battle. We learned the Americans had leased our land to build housing for their people. The land right under this house will someday be returned to my family. Father had to get permission from authorities to walk on his own land.

"One day, I went with Father to the cave. Our treasures were there. I cried when I took the obi out of the jar. I cried for all the young women who would never marry and have children. I never again wore the obi. Now that you have honored the obi by having the screen made, I tell you its story. I will miss you, Mama-San. I will miss Tracy and Duncan and Kerry. They are like the children I never had. I will miss the commander. He is a good husband and father. I send the obi to America so you will still have me with you."

We stood. She bowed from the waist, "Sayonara, my friend."

My arms ached to hug her but I knew I must not invade her dignity. I bowed in return, "I am honored. I will remember you every time I look at the screen, and I will carry you in my heart. *Domo arigato gozaimusu*, Mura-San Matsuzaki."

Marilyn Pate

Part of the Navy Means Saying Good-Bye

Cherish your human connections: your relationships with friends and family.

Barbara Bush

For most military families, a moving van idling in the street is both a regularly occurring event and a dreaded sight. It's daunting when the van is sitting outside your own house and men are carrying your dismantled belongings to the truck, but it's downright depressing when the van is waiting outside the home of your best friend.

My best girlfriend moved last week. Darcy's husband was transferred across the country to a new branch of service. I find this hard to believe, and it is difficult to accept that she is gone. But what's confusing and sad for me is traumatic for my two-and-a-half-year-old son, Ford. For the past two years, he grew up with my friend's children. Her youngest is just two weeks older than mine, and her eldest is four. I call them "The Crew." They were always together, as good as second families for one another while our husbands were deployed.

Darcy lived three houses away from me. Sometimes, while our husbands were gone, I felt like I was back at college. I would run down the street in sweatpants, with a stack of DVDs under my arm, ready for a night of girl talk and movie marathons.

How many times did I dash between our houses for a cup of milk for a recipe or to cry on her couch? I cannot be sure, but I know it measured in the hundreds. I wouldn't be surprised if I had worn a groove in the pavement between our two homes. She was my confidante, my buddy, the only programmed number on my telephone. She was even the one who drove me to the hospital when I was in labor with my second son. Without her, this street suddenly seems entirely too lonely.

For my son—who, in many ways, knew my friend and was around her more than he has been with his own father—she and her children were his world, his regularity. His daddy came and went on detachments and deployments, but the Joneses always lived a walk away. Now that they are gone, he is just old enough to understand we don't see them anymore, but still too young to know what "moving" really means. Every morning he asks to go play with The Crew, and when I take him to the babysitter, he still thinks he is going to Darcy's house. After all, that is what he did for the past two years.

The day my friend moved, my son and I walked down to her house to say good-bye. The furniture was already packed, and the rooms were empty. My son cried out, "Where'd the couch go? Where's the table?"

As we walked back home, my son wept and I realized then just how crazy this military life really is. I can't think of any other profession that allows grown-up families who aren't related to become so close. The fact that military families endure so much together brings us closer and makes us family. Over the last two years, to celebrate Thanksgiving dinner or the Fourth of July without the Joneses was like ostracizing an aunt or an uncle or a brother. We had bonded in a way that is so unique to military families. We had bonded through hardship, tragedy and long, lonely months.

Yesterday, my neighbor across the street moved. Her family is civilian, and we were pretty close as far as friendship goes. Our children played together, and she and I had several lunch dates and movie nights. But her departure hasn't affected me nearly as much as my fellow navy friends'. I never suffered through six months alone with my civilian neighbor. I never ran to her door crying or called her at two o'clock in the morning because I heard a strange noise in the kitchen. I never spent an entire Saturday with her; I never shared a holiday with her family. Monday through Friday, and especially Saturday and Sunday, my civilian friend had her husband and children at home.

With Darcy, my military friend, there were times when she and I only had each other. We'd sit alone on her back patio and listen to noisy neighbors celebrating the Fourth of July with a family picnic and fireworks. We spent Easter with our kids, hunting for eggs in my backyard. And at 5:00 P.M., when husbands and wives were rushing home to be together, she and I could usually be found yakking it up at the park, watching our children play and laugh . . . totally sheltered from what a "normal" family life is like.

This morning, my son asked, "Why did Darcy move, Momma?"

I paused, not sure how to answer in a way he could understand. "Honey," I explained, "Darcy and the boys moved away because their daddy got a new job. They won't live down the street, and we won't go to their house anymore. Somebody new lives in their house now."

I could tell that he still didn't understand. But I couldn't give him a better explanation. I don't understand why the navy brings such special people in and out of our lives. I don't understand why we have to leave a place just as soon as we get comfortable there.

What I do understand, and what my son will eventually realize, too, is that we never would have become this close with Darcy and her children if it hadn't been for the military. And now, for the rest of our lives, there will always be a guest bed waiting for us at the Joneses', wherever the military moves them next. And when we go there, we will always be welcomed. Like family.

Sarah Smiley

Discomboobled Military Mate

Self-expression must pass into communication for its fulfillment.

Pearl S. Buck

If you stay married to your military mate long enough, you'll eventually end up stationed in Europe. When my husband and I first moved to Bavaria, we were delighted to rent a small apartment in a quaint, little farming town near the American military post. I was ready for culture shock, but I was completely taken aback by the linguistic "discombooblement" I experienced. Culture shock implies a surprise at one's new surroundings. I wasn't shocked, I was bewildered, mystified, discomboobled, thrown into a state of confusion and feeling like a boob. I had tried to prepare myself for moving to a new country by listening to a "You Can Speak German in One Easy Lesson" tape. Being able to count to ten in a foreign language is helpful but, obviously, not enough. It is easier to eat crackers while whistling the national anthem than it is for an English speaker to make *ich* and *ach* sounds properly.

"Ackkkkk," I tried, spitting all over myself. My husband

came running to see if I had a chicken bone caught in my throat. *"Bitte,"* I said to him in German, thanking him with one of the few words I had learned.

"What's bitter?" he asked. "What did you choke on?"

"Ackkkk," I replied, in frustration.

Normally, my tongue is wagging at both ends. If silence was golden, I couldn't earn a plug nickel. Lucky for me, there are two languages: verbal and physical. Until I became more skilled at approximating the German dialect, I would have to resort to pantomime. The merchants wanted my money, so they played along. Besides, talk is cheap; I find that the supply always exceeds the demand.

I finally learned to say *"Guten Tag,"* which is "Good day" in German. No one told me, however, that Bavaria is to Germany what Texas is to the United States—pretty much a separate country. Saying "Good day" in Bavaria is like saying "Good day" in Texas. It's just not done. One says, "Howdy." And, in Bavaria, one says, *"Grüss Gott."*

I listened to the folks in my German town saying, *"Grüss Gott"* for about a week before I finally asked my German friend Wolfgang (that's German for Bubba) why everyone was so interested in each other's greased goat. The "You Can Speak German" cassette hadn't gone here. He explained, and I played along.

"Teach me to say, 'I'm just looking,' in German," I asked him. Every time I went into a store, the merchant hovered over me like an assault helicopter. I set off on my next shopping adventure with my new line.

"Yakkitty-yappin'," said the shopkeeper to me in German. I answered with the German quote I had learned from Wolfgang to let her know that I was just browsing.

The shopkeeper looked at me as if I were missing a few pickets from my fence and shooed me from her store. Later, Wolfgang told me what he had taught me to say: "I am a crazy American. I am armed. Back off and let me shop." No matter that I was only armed with charge cards.

I was so green in Germany, you could have planted me and I would have grown. I wanted to speak the native tongue, so I kept trying. I thought it might be easier to skip sentence structure and get straight to the point.

"Vee Cee?" I asked one merchant. I knew this was the way to say "WC" (water closet), and I needed to find the restroom.

"Yes," the merchant said in perfect English, "we take Visa."

I wanted to give up. This was more frustrating than eating soup with a fork.

Despite my idiom idiocy, I did quite well the first time my husband and I went out to eat. I knew I wanted water, *Wasser*, and I recognized *Salat* as salad. I was proud until my husband had to clarify another popular word. "Not donkey," he said. "That's *Danke*." There it is, folks— discombooblement: the inability to understand the people around you and their assumption that you are a boob.

Unlike me, my husband seemed to communicate quite well with the natives. Then again, his favorite local phrases sound a lot like they do back home. *"Bier!"* he'd say, confidently. And a frothy stein would always be forthcoming.

Jan Hornung

The Difference a Year Makes

*The true value of a human being can be found
in the degree to which he has attained liberation.*

Albert Einstein

We had been married for exactly thirty-three days when
my husband received the official notification phone call. I
remember everything with vivid clarity. Even though we
had both known he would be called to Iraq, it didn't scare
me until he walked around the kitchen corner and said,
"Honey, it's time."

I could never have prepared myself for what it was like
when my new husband walked out our door and out of
my life for a year. What do you say? What should you feel
at a moment like this? Do you express worry and concern,
or do you play the supportive role and pretend for a
moment that you know everything is going to be okay?

One year is more than just a time period. It is every
holiday. It is the first year of our marriage and our first
anniversary. It is thousands and thousands of memories
that will never be made together, never shared, never
reminisced about later. One year is loneliness, fear and

meals eaten alone in the quiet dark.

I worried about the time we were spending apart. Then it hit me—I would keep a journal!

Memories fade, and emotions are forgotten over time, but written testimonials last forever. What better way to stay connected than to inscribe our experiences, feelings, memories and activities into journals that we could later share and explore together?

I sent my husband his own blank journal and immediately started filling up the pages in mine. It felt like the next best thing to actually sharing those experiences with my husband. I found that I loved documenting the way I'd laughed through a new movie, or cried when I felt sad and alone. I wrote in great detail when I was upset or angry, and I spent pages imagining what our reunion would be like once the year was over.

I wrote about personal growth and milestones in my life as I explored my own strengths and weaknesses, and realized that I was sharing things I might never have vocalized.

Time passed, and my husband finally came home safely, bringing with him the journal I had sent. It was full of his year, his emotions and the struggles he had undergone. He wrote about the lessons he had learned and the astonishing experiences he had.

I read his journal the way I would read a suspenseful novel. Writing is intimate, and, even now, we bond on a deeper level when we read one another's most personal thoughts. I feel like I was a part of his year, and he was a part of mine, even though we weren't sharing a home, or even a continent.

During an experience that tested our marriage, challenged our commitments and postponed our happy ending, we found a way to laugh, cry and thrive together. And we still got our "happily ever after."

Megan Armstrong

Saying Good-Bye

Peace on the outside comes from peace on the inside; peace on the inside comes from under-standing we are all God.

Shirley MacLaine

In 1997, my husband, a U.S. Marine, packed up and pre-pared to leave for Okinawa, Japan, for one year. We had three small children at the time and had just completed three years of recruiting duty in Austin, Texas. We were now facing a twelve-month unaccompanied tour—two hardship duties back-to-back. My family was in San Antonio, so the kids and I moved the eighty miles south of Austin to live near family while my husband was gone. We spent the last few days before his departure spending time as a family, and making sure finances and important documents were all in order.

Charles's departure day finally arrived. It was a Sunday in early January, and we woke up that morning to cold gray skies. The weather seemed to be reflecting what I was feeling on the inside, but I had three little children to consider, and I knew my attitude would set the stage for the way we would handle the coming months.

That Saturday night, we had a special family night. Family night was usually on Monday evenings, but the next Monday would be without my husband. Treats always followed a fun activity, value lesson or family council. This particular night, we talked about why we were such a special family.

Our family is a Marine Corps family. That meant there were certain things we would have to do. One was to move around when they needed our marine in different units, and, sometimes, it meant not having him home for long periods of time while he did his job. We talked to the children about patriotism, serving our country and serving God. We talked about how our family would be blessed because of our service. We also discussed that God would watch over us a little closer and give us the strength and protection we would need while our daddy went to work across the Pacific Ocean. We then had yummy treats, lots of hugs and giggles and bedtime prayers.

When Sunday dawned, we attended church as usual. It seemed important to keep the day as normal as possible, but my heart was heavy, and I wanted the day to be over. I really believed all we had told the children, but the next twelve months loomed ahead of me as dark as the gray sky we had woken up to. That evening we loaded up our marine's gear and headed for the airport.

As the time grew closer for Charles to board the airplane, we gathered the kids from the windows looking out over the tarmac. Charles held our sixteen-month-old baby girl in his arms while he pulled our three-year-old son and six-year-old daughter into a group hug. The kids giggled and rubbed his chin for luck where the beginnings of a five o'clock shadow felt nice and scratchy, something they wouldn't feel for a long time. Something I hoped they wouldn't forget.

We found a somewhat empty corner of the boarding area, and the two older children stood at attention while I knelt down beside them. They had decided on a going-away song for their dad, and to show him they were ready to do their part in serving our country. My husband stood tall and strong in front of them, looking every inch a marine, even in civilian clothes. They serenaded him with the first verse of the "Marines Corps Hymn."

"From the halls of Mont-e-zu-u-ma, to the shores of Tripol-e-e-e-e." We sang low, but loud enough for him to hear, not really wanting to call attention to ourselves. I don't think that anthem ever touched Charles more than it did in those final moments in the airport waiting area.

He handed me our baby, gave one last round of hugs and kisses, and then picked up his backpack and turned and walked away.

There was no war he was going to fight, no humanitarian mission at stake. There was no parade or media attention. There was just one man, all alone, turning and walking away from the one thing that meant more to him than anything else in this world: his family.

As he walked away, it was evident that our family moment had not gone unnoticed by other passengers in the terminal waiting area. They knew, even though Charles was not in uniform, that he was a U.S. Marine leaving for duty and leaving his family.

As Charles approached the door leading to the gang-way, he turned one last time and we exchanged smiles and waves. Then he was gone.

There was not a dry eye in the house, except ours. Dad was leaving for work as usual. But it would be a little longer than usual before we would be together again.

Kelli Kirwan

The Line Ends Back There

Civilization is a method of living and an attitude of equal respect for all people.

Jane Addams

I was recalled to active duty during the Korean War, leaving my wife and son in Philadelphia until I could find suitable quarters in Tampa, Florida. Nancy knew she would be joining me sooner or later, but hadn't the slightest idea what to expect. Her knowledge of the military was limited to being able to differentiate between soldiers, sailors, marines and airmen.

In due course, she arrived in Tampa. I was subleasing an apartment until we could find something more permanent, and her only contact with the military was ironing my uniforms. She went shopping at the PX and commissary, both entirely new and strange experiences for her. So, too, was her concept of rank, with which she had barely a nodding acquaintance.

One day, as she was standing in the checkout line, her cart piled high, a lady attempted to push her own cart in front of the line. The would-be interloper announced that she was Mrs. Colonel Somebody and was in a hurry. Outraged, Nancy retorted that she was Mrs. Sergeant Blankfield and that she was in a hurry, too. The end of the line was back there, Nancy pointed out. The astonished lady sheepishly headed "back there," and waited her turn.

As years passed and Nancy became "Mrs. Colonel Blankfield," she never forgot her first experience with rank in the MacDill Air Force Base commissary. She expected no special favors or treatment, and sought none. To one and all, she was simply "Nancy."

Bill Blankfield, Col., USAF (Ret.)

Our National Anthem

Joy is what happens when we allow ourselves to recognize how good things really are.

Marianne Williamson

My husband and I had not been married long when he took me to an AAFES (Army & Air Force Exchange Service) movie theater at Fort Hood, Texas. We bought our tickets, purchased popcorn and carefully chose our seats to watch the film. The theater began to fill, and we waited for the curtain to go up.

My husband kept glancing at his watch as if he had to be somewhere, and, promptly at 1900 (7:00 P.M.), he set his soda and his popcorn aside. I was about to say something to him when the curtain began to part and I heard the sound of our national anthem being played. I scrambled to find somewhere to put my soda and popcorn, and finally made it to my feet and put my hand over my heart. This was certainly not the first time I had heard the national anthem, but it was the first time I heard it played in a theater before a movie.

I waited for the last note to sound and then looked at

my husband's smiling face. He had purposely not told me so he could see my reaction. Needless to say, the next time we went to a movie on post, I was ready to stand with pride for the playing of our national anthem.

When we moved to Germany, we continued our habit of seeing movies at the theater on post. We had only been there a few days when we went to our first film. Just as before, we bought our tickets and popcorn and made our way to our seats. We stood for the playing of our national anthem, and before we got to "by the dawn's early light," tears were streaming down my face. This was my blessed country's sacred song, but I was no longer living between her shores. Experiencing these words while standing on foreign soil lent every utterance and declaration a deeper meaning.

My heart swells with newfound pride and patriotism each time I hear the sweet strains that remind me of the price of my freedom. I am proud to be an American and even more proud to be married to a soldier who has defended my freedoms and yours for nineteen years.

Only by leaving America did I truly understand and appreciate love of country, and I now wait with great anticipation to return to the "land of the free and the home of the brave."

God bless America.

Gail Gross

My Home

What your heart thinks is great, is great. The soul's emphasis is always right.

Ralph Waldo Emerson

Even though I have had many addresses while serving my country (fourteen places over the last ten years), I have had only one home. My home moves with me wherever I am assigned to duty.

My wife Julie has long dark hair, hazel eyes and skin like ivory. When I walk through the door at the end of a long day at the base and see Julie's face and smell the sweet scent of her perfume, I know that I am home. My children are still young. My son, Daniel, is six, and my daughter, Samantha, is four. My house would not be my home without the sound of cartoons on the television, the children giggling and my family greeting me at the end of each day. Home is my family.

I dream of sending Daniel and Samantha to college. I dream of buying some property in a small town and building a house. I dream of spending my life with Julie and watching our children grow. Home is my dreams.

The blue couch Julie and I bought a few moves ago doesn't fit well in our new house, but it's part of our home now. We sit on it together, and I read to my children. Or we just sit and watch television. A friend gave us a red dinner plate a few years ago for Christmas. Along the edges of the plate, written in white letters, are the words, "You are special today." We only use the red plate on special days. Daniel ate off it on his first day of kindergarten. I ate off it on the first day of my new job. Samantha ate off it on her birthday. We all get to eat off the red plate on our birthdays. Home is familiar things.

My faith is always with me. God is always with me. I share that faith with Julie, and we try to set an example for our children. Our faith bonds our family together and strengthens our home. Home is my faith in God.

Home is more than a house you buy or an apartment you rent. Home is the heart you put into that house or apartment. The love families have for each other is what makes a home complete. When I move to my next duty station, I know my home will be with me because I'll have the love of my family with me. We'll bring the things we've collected over the years, and we'll make our next house our home. The red plate will be there, and the blue couch will be there. I'll have my family, my dreams, my faith in God—and I'll be home.

Benjamin Pigsley

The Angel Book

Helping one another is part of the religion of our sisterhood.

Louisa May Alcott

In 2002, I watched a friend named Patti Dawes walk a lap around the fitness track at Canadian Forces Base Petawawa. Patti, a young military wife, is a cancer survivor, and this symbolic victory lap was in recognition of her struggles. We were part of a team of women I had organized to participate in the Relay for Life, an all-night, twelve-hour event that is one of Canada's main fundraisers for the Canadian Cancer Society. From start to finish, a member of your team is always on the track.

I had just met Patti a few months earlier and was happy to have her join us. She is a generous, soft-spoken, gifted lady, and I had several conversations with her before this event about her bout with cancer. My heart was so happy for her as she traveled around the track with some of her friends. To show her that she had the love and support of all our team members, I presented her with a long-stemmed red rose from the whole team to carry on her victory lap. With a young family (two boys, ages three and eight), Patti had so much to be thankful for.

Just a year later, the words no one wants to hear were voiced: her cancer was back. Over the next few months, I watched the look on Patti's face change from sheer terror to reluctant acceptance. I marveled at the calm with which she faced her battle, and I admired her for the way she handled this incredibly difficult time.

To those not part of the military community, it can be hard to describe the bond that exists between military wives. As has been said many times over the years, in the military community, your friends become your family and your family becomes your friends. It's your friends that you call on in times of need because, most often, your family lives too far away to "be there" for you on a regular basis.

The walls of Patti's hospital room are covered with photos and greeting cards. Anyone who ever visited her home knew how much she loved angels, and her friends picked up on that, bringing angels as gifts to watch over her. Wherever you look in her hospital room, a wonderful collection of angels gives visitors the same comfort they give Patti, who makes it easy for friends and family to visit her by putting them instantly at ease.

Patti's friends showed just how much she means to them recently. Seven of her friends from the military community banded together, and, knowing of her love for angels, borrowed angel costumes, complete with halos and wings, and set out for Home Fires Park at CFB Petawawa along with a photographer. The setting was well chosen, since the park and monument are dedicated to military spouses and it is the first of its kind in Canada.

I happened to be sharing the hospital room as a patient with Patti when she was presented with her Angel Book. As I lay there in the next bed, I listened to her laugh as she looked at the results of their angelic photo shoot. These photos were like none I'd ever seen. The faces of her friends were filled with a genuine joy. You could tell that they were having a great time creating these special memories. Angels hugged trees, held hands around a lilac bush in full bloom, lay on the grass and sat on park benches.

I was so moved by Patti's special angels that I couldn't help but think what a wonderful keepsake calendar those photos would make. I was released from the hospital a few days later, but I couldn't stop thinking about it. The next time I visited Patti, she loved the idea. I went home and got on the computer, turning the photographs into Patti's Angel Calendar, and made one for her and each of her friends. I only had one picture of Patty herself, and I decided to use it for the cover.

The photo was taken in my home with a group of military wives. As I prepared to crop the photo to a manageable size, I realized that she had been standing in front of my Christmas tree—a tree I decorate each year with crocheted angels. And, of course, those angels were in the photo with her, telling me that they would watch over Patti, and everyone else who received the calendar born of our love for our friend.

As military wives, our hearts really do beat as one. We continue to pray for Patti as she fights this difficult battle, surrounded by all the love and support we can give her.

Dianne Collier

6

NO LIFE LIKE IT

*If the military had wanted you to
have a spouse, they would have issued
you one.*

Anonymous

The Difference

I never intended to become a run-of-the-mill person.

Barbara Jordan

When we consider the price the military pay for freedom, we need to remember the spouses. They pay a price, too. The funny thing about it is that most military spouses don't consider themselves different from other husbands and wives. Is there a difference? I think there is.

Other spouses get married and look forward to building equity in a home and putting down family roots. Military spouses get married and know they'll live in base housing or rent their homes. They must carry their roots with them, transplanting them frequently.

Other spouses decorate a home with a flair and personality that can last a lifetime. When military spouses decorate their homes, their flair is tempered with the knowledge that no two base houses have the same size windows or same size rooms. Curtains have to be flexible and multiple sets are a plus. Furniture must fit like puzzle pieces.

Other spouses have living rooms that are immaculate and seldom used. Military spouses have immaculate living-room/dining-room combos. The coffee table got a scratch or two moving from Germany, but it still looks pretty good.

Other spouses say good-bye to their spouse for a business trip and know they won't see them for a week. They are lonely, but can survive. Military spouses say good-bye to their deploying spouse and know they won't see them for months; or for a remote, a year. They are lonely, but will survive.

Other spouses call Maytag when a washer hose blows off and then write a check for the repairman. Military spouses cut the water off and fix it themselves.

Other spouses are used to saying "hello" to friends they see all the time. Military spouses get used to saying "good-bye" to friends made over the last two years.

Other spouses worry about whether their child will be class president at school next year. Military spouses worry about whether their child will be accepted in yet another new school next year; and whether that school will be the worst in the city . . . again.

Other spouses can count on spouse participation in special events: birthdays, anniversaries, concerts, football games, graduations and especially the birth of a child. Military spouses only count on each other, because they realize that the flag has to come first if freedom is to survive. It has to be that way.

Other spouses put up yellow ribbons when the troops are imperiled across the globe and take them down when the troops come home. Military spouses wear yellow ribbons around their hearts—and they never take them off.

Other spouses worry about being late for Mom's Thanksgiving dinner. Military spouses worry about getting back from Japan in time for Dad's funeral.

Other spouses are touched by the television program showing an elderly lady putting a card down in front of a long, black wall that has names on it. The card simply says, "Happy birthday, sweetheart. You would have been sixty today." A military spouse is the lady with the card. And the wall is the Vietnam Memorial.

I would never say military spouses are better or worse than other spouses. But I will say there is a difference. And I will say that our country asks more of military spouses than is asked of other spouses. And I will say, without hesitation, that military spouses pay just as high a price for freedom as do their active-duty husbands or wives. Perhaps the price they pay is even higher. They do what they have to do, bound together not only by blood or friendship, but with a shared spirit whose origin is in the very essence of what love truly is. Dying in service to our country is not nearly as hard as loving someone who has died in service to our country, and having to live without them.

God bless our military spouses for all they freely give. And God bless America.

Col. Steven A. Arrington

Wow

Pleasure is always derived from something out-side you, whereas joy arises from within.

Eckhart Tolle

It's no big deal. It's only six months. We've been through this before! I must have told myself this a thousand times over the last six months. Now the day is here. As I drive through the ribbon-festooned streets of Camp Lejeune to the reunion site, my heart is pounding and my stomach is jumpy. I glance down at my clothes and wonder if they complement my figure. I check my makeup in the mirror and wipe the mascara that is already running.

Finally, I find a place to park and see that the crowd is forming. No definite time, no surprise, just a cattle call for between ten and six. (I was there at nine.) It's June, and it's *hot.* I see a friendly face and take a seat. The usual conversation begins. "Are you excited?" "What do you think he's going to say?" "When did you talk to him last?" You see, to some, six months is long; to others, six months is longer. Of course I am excited. I have no idea what he's going to say! The last question, I think, was to check up on her husband. If mine called me, why didn't hers call her? (I've been there.)

There's always something new to tell or show someone after half a year: a new bedspread, a new pet, a new baby. Oh, yeah, did I forget to mention that I'm nine months pregnant? My friend had a baby the month after our husbands left. We were both scared. That jumpy stomach feeling is back. Our little girl can sense my anxiety. Now I'm regretting that Pop-Tart.

As I glance down at the woman's small baby, I start to cry again. At least my husband will be here in time to see her born. Ouch! Okay, not funny—contraction! Just a Braxton-Hicks one, I know, but still, wouldn't that be something? "Well, honey, you almost made it in time!" I grab a drink of water, to take the edge off, or does that saying only apply to hard liquor?

I didn't sleep much last night, and although it's bright and hot, I find myself starting to doze. I take one more look down the parking lot: no buses. As soon as I start to close my eyes, someone screams; now I hear laughter. I snap my eyes open and look again: still nothing. I notice everyone is looking in the opposite direction. It's a dirt road and there are three big trucks and a line of buses coming up from behind for a sneak attack. It works!

Well, my nap long forgotten, I jump up—okay, not jump, more like awkwardly slide—out of my chair. After much scrambling and waddling about, I decide it will be much easier if I stand still. So, I wait by the sea of green sea bags. I run my fingers through my hair and smooth my new pink shirt over my belly, and then I remember. *Oh no! I'm pregnant!* For some absurd reason, I try to suck in my gut. All I achieve by that is to anger the baby, and am punished by a swift kick to the ribs and a head butt to the bladder. Note to self: *Don't try that again.* So, I stand there and wait.

Finally, the mass of green camouflage starts to thin as other wives snatch their husbands out of line. Over someone's head, I see familiar eyes. Exactly the same, yet somehow different. It could be that he's tanned, or, no . . . tears?! Surely not. But as he draws closer I see him bite his lower lip. It's true! As if in an old movie, time slows down. I see his eyes flicker to my stomach and widen. I search for something profound to say, and I'm sure he does as well. All I can do is protectively place my hands over my baby and hope her daddy doesn't turn away and run screaming at the impending responsibility. He does just the opposite. He drops his bags and pulls my body as close as possible and whispers a small but heartfelt word: "Wow."

Amy Hollingsworth

The Delivery of Finding Strength

Giving birth is little more than a set of contractions granting passage of a child. Then the mother is born.

Erma Bombeck

"I can't believe you went to work with your water broken!" The nurse ordered me to the hospital immediately. "You are too strong! Get down here, now."

Cradling the phone, I thought about what she had said. "Too strong" were not words that I had ever associated with myself. She had not seen me at home during the past five months, wanting my husband desperately, wondering how on earth I was going to deliver this precious baby without my partner by my side. Even though it was not wartime, Joe was halfway across the country, completing engineer officer basic course, and was not allowed to come back for the birth of our daughter without having to start the course over. We had already decided months prior to his leaving that he would stay there and be able to return when our baby girl was a few weeks old. Easier said than done! I was beginning to regret that decision.

I called my mother-in-law and gathered my things. As I walked down the hall of the school, my students cheered, while I wondered how long this would take and how quickly I could get word to Joe.

After picking some things up at home, I was off to the hospital, where the maternity ward was full. This was typical. Nothing in my life has come easy! So I labored here, there and everywhere until a delivery room opened up. This was painful. Having my son had been a walk in the park compared to this. Joe had been so wonderful through the birth of our son, coaching, comforting and joking. I was pretty much flying solo this time. Yes, my sister-in-law and mother-in-law were with me, and I was thankful for them, but I craved my husband's warmth, encouragement and strength. I could barely stop crying with wishing that Joe was with me. Then the phone rang.

"Hi, babe! How are you doing?" said my sweet husband. "I wish I could be with you. I love you! You're doing great!"

My spirits soared! My soldier had gotten the message, and knew just what to do to "be with me." The epidural took effect, and I actually slept through the hardest part of the birth. Sweet dreams of my camouflaged hero coming home took over. There he was, holding our baby girl and five-year-old son, hugging me. . . .

"Honey, it's time to push," were the words that awakened me a few hours later. And push I did! Just after midnight, our beautiful Kaitlin Rose was born, looking identical to her brother and dad. Shortly after, another phone call came. It was the proud papa!

"I just know my baby girl and beautiful wife are perfect in every way! Thank you, Kim, for being so strong," he exclaimed.

This was the second time in a day that I had been told that I was strong. A calm, peaceful, quiet and proud feeling came over me. It was all going to be all right! I really could do this! I *had* done this!

All along, I thought I was a marshmallow. It took a difficult situation to teach me that I was actually a rock. Now that my husband is deployed overseas in Iraq, I ponder this remarkable turning point in my life and thank God above for helping me to come to this realization. My children and soldier husband will be depending on me to call upon that inner strength quite often in the months to come. I will, for I am an army wife—a very proud, very strong, army wife.

Kimberly L. Shaffer

Operation Enduring Freedom

There are two ways to live your life. One is as though nothing is a miracle, the other as if everything is a miracle.

Albert Einstein

E-mail has changed the military wife's daily operations during deployments. In World War II, most had to rely on what we now refer to as snail mail, which could take months each way. Now, we have this glorious and almost instant communication to keep us together. During his last deployment to Pakistan, my husband and I kept in touch this way every few days. I would tell him about his then eight-month-old son and all that was new or funny or sad with him. He would tell me what he could about life in the Middle East, which was next to nothing.

During one tough week, I had our baby at the doctor's office five or six times. Upon reading this, Daniel asked me how he could ever repay me. This was my response:

"Well, you can never repay me. You will never get back these days that your son grew without you watching. You can never go back and hug me when I was feeling my loneliest or most frustrated, no matter how many millions of hugs you are planning for me upon your return. You will never know what the eighth, ninth and tenth months of your first child's development were like. You can't ever witness those firsts: the first time he kissed, the first time he climbed, the first time he chewed food. . . .

"You can never repay me, just as I can never repay you. No matter how many times I say thank you, it won't be enough for the endless days of endless heat. No matter how many flags I fly or prayers I say or votes I cast, it won't be enough to make up for the freedoms and liberties you sacrificed for mine. No matter how many nights I stay up with our son, it won't rival the numbers of night skies you soar, keeping watch over a distant land that poses a threat to your homeland.

"Yes, it is hard to be without you. If you were a businessman on a trip, it would be hard to be without you. Yes, I worry about you, and I worry about us without you. No, it isn't easy to be the ones left behind. In fact, I was feeling a little bad about it today, after a particularly bad night with Zaden and his impending teeth, when I received an e-mail with a picture of soldiers (the lucky ones) sleeping. Sleeping, they were, on the sand, in full gear, with masks over their faces because of the dust.

"All of a sudden, I was ashamed at my ungratefulness, and so thankful for my bed and pillow, and the blanket of security that they were affording me by giving up their own. I get a bed, a house and a sand-free life. I get to kiss our baby, get to feel his soft skin on my lips. I get to hug him and hold him and rock him. I get to sit at complete peace while he lies in my arms and contentedly sucks on a bottle. I get to smell him every day. I get to listen to him babble and to laugh. I get to be with him.

"You get to sleep on a cot, if it's not too hot or too noisy. You get to carry a radio and be on alert. You get to watch your friends die in a helicopter crash. You get to attend their memorials. You get to open America in a small box that was mailed weeks ago. You get three months of trying, harsh conditions, the full extent of which I will never understand.

"If I ever complain about my situation, it will happen in a moment of weakness and selfishness, and I will be wrong to do it. The truth is that I am very proud of you. I am proud of who you are and what you chose to do for a living. I am in awe of your selflessness. I am in your debt forever, and I know it.

"I love you to the ends of the earth, and I just hope that's enough to encompass your current twenty."

Heidi Boortz

Hair Humor

We either make ourselves miserable, or we make ourselves strong. The amount of work is the same.

Carlos Castaneda

I've been burned, blonded, streaked, foiled, bobbed, stripped, layered, shaved, treated, ironed and turned into a brunette—all in the name of beauty. It's been part of my journey on the U.S. military-wife hairstyle circuit, and one of the treats of being married to a serviceman. Every time we get PCS orders, panic strikes not only my heart, but my hair as well. You know when your husband walks in the door with "The Look" that soon you will not only be unpacking hundreds of mislabeled boxes in a new home, but you will also be on the adventure of looking for a new stylist. And, after five distinctly different haircuts and finding the stylist who finally suits you in the ninety-mile vicinity of your new home, your husband comes home with "The Look" again, and you know you're soon off on another hair-raising adventure.

In the past eighteen years, my hairdressers, stylists and beautifiers have come in all shapes and sizes. I've had a chic English lady in a Tudor-style salon; a manic-depressive former hippie who is married with children; a cigar-smoking, gum-cracking beauty parlor owner who kept special punch going in a special bowl for special customers. They've made me laugh, cry, pout and pray.

I laughed out loud and almost ran screaming from the salon when the nice owner told me she had been to "beauty training" forty-nine years ago and was so happy that this state did not require a license to cut hair any-more, only to do permanent waves.

I cried the day I heard, "Oh, here, let me fix that. It'll grow, you know. Things grow much faster in the South. And, by the way, honey, if you say you want short hair in the South, you're gonna get short!"

I became increasingly annoyed from the pulsating pain and the words, "Hmmmm, I'm so very sorry I burnt your forehead. I've never done that before giving a perm. In all my years working in the beauty industry here at the mall, I've never seen a welt like that! Must be some chemical in your hair from that last place you lived. Maybe you better get on the Internet and check into that."

I pouted for a week after they said, "Brown? Oh, I thought you said blonde. Well, don't worry now because this is only semipermanent and it should wash out in about three months."

But now, after all these years, I have decided to forget the crying, the weeklong irritability and the pouting. I have decided to use my time to get acquainted with these beauty folks and learn about their lives, really listen to them and encourage them in their life journeys.

The stories I have heard range from amusing to down-right depressing. One woman regaled me with her hus-band's tales of "hunting for deer in the woods." Some of my stylists have been forgotten, mistreated or divorced. One didn't know how he would pay for his health insurance.

Several have never moved more than a block away from their family homes. Thanks to Uncle Sam and the U.S. Air Force, my life truly is an adventure to them—I'm remembered, insured, treated well, travel extensively and still very much in love with my husband!

Instead of expecting these beauty folks to wave a magic wand and make me beautiful for $19.99 plus the tip, I now wonder if I've been more than just an irritable customer, passing through town on a three-year tour. Have I been a friend? Have I been a good ambassador for our air force?

Instead of feeling sorry for myself when my husband comes home with "The Look," I remind myself how quickly assignments pass, how quickly our lives pass through others' lives, and how I have an opportunity to be kind, to laugh, to pray, to be a lady.

We're all different, but we're the same, too. We all have fears and foibles, faults and favorites. I can choose to enjoy this journey, to learn from my experiences and all the people God sprinkles into my life. Or I can be miserable. I have the opportunity in that sea foam swivel chair (wearing the lovely matching sea foam frilly cape) to learn and listen, laugh and encourage. My hair, my choice, my attitude.

Laura C. Fitch

Footsteps at the Door

Another sleepless night for me
Alone upon our bed
I see again his every move
And those last words he said.

So proud he looked in uniform
Convinced that he was right
He had to go, for duty called
There was a war to fight.

Those last few days before he left
I hid the pain inside
We talked and loved and even joked
He never knew I cried.

And when the dreaded moment came
He kissed me tenderly
His eyes met mine, and then he said,
"I'll be all right, you'll see."

I tried to smile and nod my head
Afraid to let him see
The terror that I feared if he
Did not come back to me.

His precious children hugged his neck
He told them to be good
And help their mommy out at home
And mind her like they should.

They were too young to realize
That Dad would not be there
To tuck them in their beds at night
Or listen to their prayers.

I see him as he walked away
I tried to say "good-bye"
But words were trapped within my throat
All I could do was cry.

The weeks have stretched now into months
And every night I pray
That God will keep him in his care
And bring him home one day.

I do not moan beneath the load
Of all that I must do
My children will see strength in me
Until this war is through.

At last I drift off into sleep
In dreams I see him more
I turn around and smile to hear
His footsteps at the door.

Restless I sleep, and then I wake
Not opening my eyes
I move my hand to reach for him
But no one near me lies.

I will not give in to despair
With each new day I'll cope
For I know he would want me to
Be brave and live with hope.

I hear the voices loud and strong
Who criticize the war
While yelling men are fools to go
They stay on freedom's shore.

A man who cowers under fear
Will die a thousand deaths
While men like mine for freedom fight
And offer their last breaths.

I hope perhaps in fifty years
When men remember war
They won't forget the wives who dreamed
Of footsteps at the door.

Gwen C. Rollings

Only Joking

Ask and it shall be given to you.

Matthew 7:7

I was a military wife stationed in California in the mid-1980s. My helicopter pilot husband was gone much of the time. He handled the separations in his way, and I handled them in mine.

During this time, he was often in Panama for three to four months at a time. He was able to call me at home once a week, for five minutes. I was often not at home when he phoned and would keep his messages on the answering machine tape to listen to over and over again until he returned.

Once, just before he was due to return, he phoned, and during the conversation said he had bought something for me. The very next night he was able to surprise me with another phone call. He had only a minute to talk, saying he had been celebrating the night before and didn't remember what we'd talked about. I reminded him that he said he'd bought me lace table linens and a gold bracelet. He hung up before I could tell him that I was only joking and that he hadn't told me what he'd bought for me at all.

When he got home three days later and was emptying his duffel bag, there they were: the hand-embroidered lace tablecloth and napkins, and a lovely gold bracelet— all of which he had quickly gone out and bought for me after that second phone call.

I finally told him the truth about that second phone call, but only after I'd put the linens on the table and the bracelet on my wrist. We had a good laugh, and he never again used his five-minute phone call to telephone me after he'd been "celebrating."

Vicki A. Vadala-Cummings

"Tell me again about the time you helped to
fortress a city, subdue hostile fire and got home
and baked us all raspberry strudels."

Thank You

Just to be is a blessing. Just to live is holy.

Rabbi Abraham Heschel

During my husband's yearlong deployment to Iraq, we received many words of encouragement from friends, family and a surprising number of strangers. In fact, it was a person I had never met who gave me the boost I needed to endure the long separation and endless, worrisome nights.

In Iraq, part of Brian's job was to locate contractors to make necessary repairs to the public facilities in his unit's area of responsibility. One of those facilities was the Hiba Down's Syndrome School. It was a school founded by Mr. and Mrs. Mansur, whose daughter Hiba was born with Down's syndrome. The school had been damaged in the war, and the teachers hadn't been paid in several months.

Brian visited the Hiba school frequently to ensure that the repairs were being done and that all the needs of the school were addressed. On one particular visit, he had the great pleasure of giving paychecks to the teachers and Mrs. Mansur, the headmistress. He told me about the joy and gratitude they expressed to him on that day. In fact, with that little bit of money, Mrs. Mansur purchased a small wrapped package, which she gave to Brian on his next visit. But the gift was not for him. Instead, she instructed Brian to send the little gift to me.

Me?! What did I do? Nothing! I just stayed here hoping and praying that Brian would survive another day. The gift wasn't anything expensive or exotic. It was a simple bracelet and necklace made of the thinnest metal I had ever seen. But the short handwritten note that accompanied the gift brings tears to my eyes each time I think of it. It read: "Thank you for your husband." That is the kind of encouragement we all need. We know that it's worth it; it's just nice to hear that somebody else appreciates it.

Kristin Spurlock

The Cookie Lady

Everything we say and do has an effect on the fabric of humanity.

Mahatma Gandhi

As the events of 9/11 unfolded on TV, I did not realize what that meant for our little military community in Mountain Home, Idaho. Within hours, our lives as we knew them changed drastically as word spread of the possible deployment of our squadron in support of Operation Enduring Freedom. Within a week, that word came true, and members of our squadron began deploying.

For security reasons, spouses are not immediately told where their loved ones are going or for how long. The good-byes were especially hard as this was a "first" for many in our young squadron.

The day my husband left, I found a Baggie of cookies hanging on my mailbox. A note was attached with black and red ribbon, our squadron colors, which read: "Thinking of you, Linda!" As I looked at the note trying to recognize the handwriting, I turned it over and saw one of the squadron patches photocopied on the back and realized this person had gone to a bit of trouble to do this. I enjoyed every cookie and wondered who had thought of me.

As the first week went by and Friday was approaching, I was thinking about our first weekend without my husband and how lonely it would be for our children and myself. I woke up Friday to another Baggie of cookies! The note attached read: "Here's a Friday cookie pick-me-up for you!"

By then, there was a rumor that a young captain's wife in our squadron, Julie, was the one spreading good cheer to all the spouses in our squadron living on the base. We loved it! She was dubbed "The Cookie Lady." Every Friday, there was a different kind of cookie hanging from my mailbox with a word of encouragement attached. I so looked forward to Fridays! Even my children would ask what kind of cookies I got today. That little gesture of kindness kept us all going in a time of uncertainty for our husbands as well as our nation.

Our spouses were deployed for four months, and, every Friday during that time, Julie baked and delivered cookies to the spouses. The last cookie delivery she made was to our husbands after they arrived home safely from the deployment. The note attached read: "We are proud of you and the job you've done to serve our country! Welcome home!"

Linda Valle

The Honeymoon Is Over

If your ship doesn't come in, swim out to it.

Jonathan Winters

In the spring of 1963, I brought my new bride of three weeks home to meet my parents. We had to stretch the fifty dollars we had to get home to Redwood City, 475 miles away, where money in my bank account was waiting.

We had to select from two motels on either side of the highway. One wanted fifteen dollars for the night, while the other wanted four dollars. I opted for the bargain, but my wife wanted to stay where the amenities were more conducive to "freshening up" and looking her best when she was introduced to my family.

I pointed out the practical side of the situation— notably, the lack of funds—so she reluctantly agreed on the bargain.

I'd just set our bags down when my wife noticed the busy scurrying of a multitude of tiny black "critters" cavorting on the shag throw rug next to the bed!

Wanting to make the best of a sticky situation, I took the rugs outside and gave them a good shake, then placed them back on the floor. "Oh, no!" she said. "I don't want those filthy things in here!"

"Okay, honey," I replied and put them outside by the door. I wasn't about to dispute the matter further because she was clearly agitated.

After a few kisses and an apology from me, she snuggled up and said, "Oh, that's okay. I know we have to save money, and it's really not so bad."

Young love is great, isn't it? That was about to change—drastically.

"Why don't you go get some takeout while I shower and wash my hair?"

Good idea, I thought. It would give her some time to cool down a bit, for she was still a tad upset.

I returned from the greasy spoon with two hamburgers and two helpings of fries in a grease-stained paper sack to be greeted by pounding and crying coming from the bathroom.

"The water just stopped; I've got my hair and eyes full of shampoo; there's no towels in here and I can't open the door because somehow it's locked. Just get me out of here. Please!" she said.

I turned the knob but it wouldn't budge. I shook it, rattled the door and did everything I could to get it to open—all to no avail. Giving one last mighty turn, I felt a grinding from within, and the knob came off in my hand as its mate dropped to the floor on the other side.

We replaced the knobs on the door, but no amount of fiddling would get the stubborn thing to open.

"Sorry, honey, I'll have to get the manager."

"But I don't have any clothes on. . . ."

"Just stay calm, dear."

The manager, a grizzled old geezer, wearing a pair of stained overalls, dusty brown high-top boots, and a T-shirt that, even in its better days, should have been used as a dust rag, was very helpful and understanding.

"Well, ain't that somethin'!" he exclaimed as he turned the knob to no avail.

He threw up his hands. "Hang on. I'll be right back."

"Everything will be fine, honey," I said through the door as she sobbed. "Just be a little patient, okay?"

Soon the manager returned and handed me a fire ax. "Just break it down. Don't worry about damages. Should have fixed that a long time ago."

"Stand back, honey!" I said.

"What are you doing?" my wife screamed as the first of several blows from the heavy ax split open the door.

"Getting the door open, love," I replied. "Just stay calm, okay?"

In short order, the door was in splinters, and my disheveled wife emerged with drying soap clinging to her wet hair, and I couldn't help but chuckle at the sight.

I soon learned a husband should never confront his wife with laughter, especially when she doesn't look her best. I swore I wasn't laughing at her, just at the situation. Yet at the time my sensitive mate took it personally. She said nothing to me. She didn't have to. Her eyes said it all!

I returned the ax to the manager and asked about the water. "How is my wife going to get the soap out of her hair?"

The old guy scratched the back of his head for a moment, then brightened. "Wal, there's a fifty-gallon barrel that collects rainwater from the gutters. Ain't rained for a bit, but she's welcome to use it."

The condition of the water in the barrel made the rugs look like Persian carpets. All sorts of debris and bugs were collected at the top. Some living, most dead.

Enough is enough, I thought. The fancy motel was beginning to look like a bargain. If we didn't eat breakfast and had crackers for lunch, we could make it home on thirty-five dollars.

We were lying in bed at the "expensive" motel when I turned to her and chuckled. "Y'know, love, a few years from now we'll look back on all of this and laugh."

No comment.

The following day a beautiful and elegant Lynne emerged from the car to welcome hugs from my mother and father.

Forty-two years later, we're still happily married with three children, eight grandchildren and fifteen years of military service. However, I had never really apologized for my wrong decision. Now I realized that girl of twenty-one years simply wanted to please her man.

One evening, I took her in my arms and hugged her.

"I'm sorry, dear."

She turned toward me with a puzzled look on her face and frowned. "For what?"

"Motel Hell. Guys can really be insensitive, I know. I was no exception."

She snuggled into my shoulder, her lips close to my ear. "It was something," she said.

"Yeah," I replied. And this time we *both* laughed.

Gary Luerding

It'll Be Okay

On the evening of December 17, 1981, Red Brigade terrorists broke into an apartment in Verona, Italy, and kidnapped U.S. Army Brigadier General James L. Dozier. Two weeks later, as my wife, Nita, and I and our two small daughters were traveling to our home in a small village not far from there, a car raced alongside, matched its speed with ours, took a flash photo, and sped away. Although I took a zigzag course home, a second car attempted to follow us into our driveway. I slammed the gate shut and locked it, and after hurrying my wife and two wide-eyed little ones into the house, quickly reported the incident.

Because documents taken from General Dozier's apartment identified my position as commander of a nearby unit, U.S. military and Italian police decided to take no chances. After sifting through the possibilities, the next morning, the entire family was moved on thirty minutes' notice.

There might have been a brief catch in Nita's voice when I called her with the news. If so, it was replaced in an instant with understanding, strength and a closing of "It'll be okay"—despite having just been told that she had a half-hour to pack for a move of indefinite duration to a place not yet determined. Nita asked the girls to help by choosing the items they wished to take with them. It has since become part of our family legend that Laura, our twelve-year-old, only packed her records. Fortunately, Nita did a last-minute logistics check and suggested that perhaps things like clothes, toothbrushes and shoes might also be useful.

We were taken to a guarded "safe haven" area on a military post. When the news of the incident reached my boss in Germany, he called to ask if I wanted to leave, to be reassigned elsewhere either temporarily or permanently. After I declined his well-meant offer, he asked if he should move my family—perhaps bring them to Germany for a while.

We talked about it that night in the small apartment that was our "safe haven" home. Around a tiny table in the kitchen, with the windows shuttered and barred, and an armed guard outside our door, we held a family conference. I explained the offer that had been presented to us. Nita gave me a "you must be kidding" look, said she and the kids would be staying, and resumed reading her novel. We remained in the "safe haven" for forty-two days, until the *carabinieri* (the Italian military police) freed General Dozier from his captors.

Many years have passed since that ominous night in Italy. I think about it often in light of the countless numbers of American military families now placed in peril all around the globe. Somehow, I believe that military members forced by circumstances to make one of those phone calls will get responses from their spouses that sound much like Nita's reply to me all those years ago. The voice on the line will be strong and understanding—and the conversation will close with "It'll be okay."

Tom Phillips

7

UNITED
WE STAND

The greatest formal talent is worthless if it does not serve a creativity which is capable of shaping a cosmos.

Albert Einstein

Sacrifices

Just remember, we're all in this alone.

Lily Tomlin

"So, you're a military wife?"

This doesn't sound too flattering coming from a civilian who has no concept of military life. My father was a marine for thirty-one years, and I married a marine. When I said, "I do," twenty-six years ago, I knew what I was getting into. Most people don't understand what it takes. They don't realize that we, the spouses, are just as involved. We make more sacrifices in twenty years than most people do in a lifetime.

We wring our hands when our husbands don't come home some evenings, knowing they might be on spontaneous maneuvers, but no one will tell us for sure. So we sit and wait, gripped with the fear that when the door opens, we'll see a captain standing there in his dress blues, his cover in his hand and regret in his eyes. It wasn't "playing marine" this time. It was for real. We imagine the things we might say to our children if we ever had to have those conversations.

From Desert Shield to Desert Storm to Operation Iraqi Freedom, the nation needed the Corps and it was there—trained, ready and willing to give the ultimate sacrifice. The world witnessed the support that has always been there, in us, the other half of the Corps.

I get a lump in my throat when I hear the "Marine Corps Hymn" or the "Star Spangled Banner." My shoulders pull back and my chin lifts a little higher when I see my husband in his uniform or when someone asks me what he does for a living and I say with great pride, "He's a United States Marine."

I heard a civilian woman say to my mother, "Oh, how fortunate are military families: free housing, medical and dental care, the commissary. . . ." My mother replied, "Nothing is free. It's compensation."

It's compensation when they take the husband, the father, and, more often now, the mother and wife, for a year at a time to serve in some remote location that's strategic and secret and has no name. Yet, it's little compensation when you pass by a house after a terrorist attack on the marine barracks—and see a black wreath hanging from the door. You know inside there is a widow with children. And I know that widow could have been me.

The marine wife is a special breed. She's a strong woman. I owe a lot of my strength to my mother. I saw her cope with hardships that would have made any man fold.

What would you do if you found yourself stranded in a New Jersey airport in ninety-degree weather with three children under the age of five, dressed for your destination in Iceland with no passports, no lodging, no luggage and no help? I'm proud to say she overcame this and we met my father in Iceland, a little ragged—but together.

Mom showed me how to look for things that most people don't see: the young marine away from home during the holidays, missing those home-cooked meals in a family surrounding, or the expectant mother who is frightened and wishing her mom was close so she could ask her questions she thinks might be silly.

We take care of our own, and hope that when our loved ones are in a similar situation, someone will reciprocate. Giving thanks takes such a small effort.

A point of advice to young marine wives: seek the support of other marine wives, enlisted or officer or in the links program. Experience is the best teacher. They were in your shoes once before and know what you are feeling. Ask. They know all you need to know: the tricks to a smoother moving day, quarter inspection, medical facilities, the schools and definitely the best shops. And if they don't know the answer to your specific question, you can be certain they'll know where to find it.

If I sound as if I'm glorifying the marine family, perhaps I am. We're just as good at what we do as our marines are. We are not simply wives and husbands and children. We are a part of the marine team.

Amy J. Fetzer

Dreams and Doubts

I don't care how long he is away from home, as long as he comes home.

Karin Mercendetti

June 10, 1944. The lunch rush was over, and a sharp gust of wind slammed the door shut behind the last customer. Sophia poured a cup of coffee, dished up the last piece of homemade apple pie and sat down. Instead of eating, she stared out the window and prayed with all her heart that her beloved husband would give her a sign that he was still alive. She felt in her heart that he was fine, but a little voice inside kept questioning that feeling.

They had met when she was only fifteen and working in a hospital after school. He was five years older, handsome, charming, brilliant and fun. They became friends instantly, but waited four years to get married. They scrimped and saved for five more years to fulfill their dream of buying their own business, this small hotel and restaurant on the river in Gowanda, New York. Since their wedding, they had not been apart for a night, until he went into the army.

She found herself remembering the day that Vic had received his draft notice. It was on his birthday, and she was devastated. Why did they want a married thirty-two-year-old? The notice, however, didn't faze Vic. He was eager to serve his country.

Vic had wanted with all of his heart to be a pilot because he had enjoyed flying a friend's airplane around the countryside near their home every chance he got. But the army made him a staff sergeant in the mess hall because of his culinary skills. (He said there wasn't much you could do with powdered eggs and dried beef!)

He had been moved to several different bases in the South during the past nineteen months. Sophia had taken the train to visit him several times and enjoyed the graciousness of the people, but not the oppressive heat and humidity. She was content that she had remained at home to take care of their business instead of trying to follow him from base to base. With help from her younger sister Josephine, she ran the hotel and restaurant quite efficiently, managing to build a substantial nest egg.

The war seemed to go on endlessly, but Vic had just been home on leave a few weeks ago. He was excited about his current assignment where he had learned to fly something called a glider plane. He went on and on with details that she didn't comprehend, but his enthusiasm was so contagious that she listened attentively. He had informed her that he would be going to Europe within days. He allayed her fears for his safety by talking about their hopes and dreams for the future. He was convinced that the war would end soon, and they talked of moving to the big city to buy a larger business and having a child when he returned.

But would he return? Now she wasn't so sure. It had been four days since she had seen the front page of the newspaper with the horrible news of all the glider pilots killed in the D-day invasion of France. She didn't know for sure where he was, but she could put two and two together! The government couldn't, or wouldn't, confirm his whereabouts. Her fingers nervously twirled her wedding ring, and she prayed again for a sign that he was okay. She sipped the now-cold coffee and took a bite of the apple pie.

And then she saw them. Two soldiers in uniform were standing and talking next to a green Jeep parked a few buildings down the block. Terror gripped her heart and she prayed like she had never prayed before. . . . *No, God! Please, no!*

They started walking toward the hotel. They were coming inside. The place was empty at two-thirty in the afternoon. She was riveted in place, staring at them. She couldn't speak. Her chest tightened, and she winced at the sharp pain from squeezing her wedding ring too hard.

They kept walking toward her. Finally, one of them said, "Can we get a couple of beers?"

A wave of relief washed over her as she delivered the drinks and said the beers were on the house. She explained to them that her husband was missing in action, and she initially thought they were bringing her bad news.

The next morning, the phone rang at five and she picked it up to hear the operator asking if she would accept a collect call. "Thank you, God!" she exclaimed. "Oh Vic, you really are alive! I knew it. I just knew it." Vic explained that he was still in Georgia and had been injured during a final training exercise. He ended up in the infirmary and couldn't go on to France and fly the gliders with his squadron. He was disappointed and ashamed that he had not gone on to fulfill his dream.

Communications hadn't been good in the infirmary, and he just now learned of the hundreds of friends lost when the gliders landed in France. However, something kept whispering to him that he needed to contact his wife. Since there were no phones on the base that he could use, it had been several days before he was able to get a ride into town to call her.

What amazed both of them the most was how they had been expressing their feelings and "speaking to each other" without a word, while they were hundreds of miles apart.

Sophia Shell
As told to Cindy Shell Pedersen

Bluegrass Parkway

Our humanity is a poor thing were it not for the divinity which stirs within us.

Sir Francis Bacon

As an army wife of twelve years, I am no stranger to taking long road trips with our two boys. But a year full of ups and downs amidst numerous separations had left me feeling like my tank was already on empty at the start of my husband's latest deployment to the Middle East.

The prospect of driving from Fort Campbell, Kentucky, to visit family in New Jersey was overwhelming and filled me with dread. I tried to talk myself out of the trip, but I knew it was important for the boys to spend time with family they had not seen in a year.

As the date for our trip drew near, my husband seemed to sense my anxiety when he called from Iraq, and he did everything he could do to make our trip easier for me. He e-mailed directions, tried to find things for the boys and me to do along the way and sent words of encouragement via e-mail.

The week before the trip was extremely hectic. There

were the usual responsibilities, the kids were going crazy with missing their dad, and I got sick. My friends thought I should postpone the trip. I was tempted.

We finally got on the road late in the day on a Tuesday in June. As I searched for the next road change, I glanced over at the passenger seat fully expecting to see my husband sitting there, a map spread across his lap, navigating our way as he usually would on our trips. My heart sank at the sight of the empty seat, and, in spite of myself, I fought tears. *What am I doing?* I was overwhelmed with a longing for him, and the sleepless nights were catching up with me. I wanted to just turn around and go home. I began to pray and to try to focus on all the ways God shows us we are never really alone.

Just as I found the Kentucky Bluegrass Parkway, the boys really needed to find a restroom. I got off at the next exit onto what turned out to be a stretch of mountain road with no gas stations or restaurants. I turned around to go on to the next exit, but there was no return ramp going east on the parkway. We drove up and down the road to be sure we hadn't missed a sign, and when we came upon a small church with cars in the parking lot, I decided to ask for some help.

We entered through a side door and found a lively group of ladies, some sewing and ironing, some setting out a pot-luck dinner. They immediately tried to feed us, and several ladies gave me directions. It made me happy just to be near them all. When I laughingly explained that I was turned around because my navigator was in Iraq, they gathered into a circle and prayed for George and the others serving to protect our freedoms. They prayed for the "stranger God sent to us" and for our children and our trip. Then they went a step further and escorted us back to the parkway to continue safely on our way.

Suddenly, the drudgery of the trip disappeared. My

heart soared at the sight of the clouds and the mountains and the beauty of God's love as shown through those ladies. I wasn't so overwhelmed or tired or lonely. I felt the pride of loving a man as selfless and giving as my husband. I thought about the joy our children bring and of all the blessings in our lives. I began to truly enjoy the drive, and the passenger seat didn't seem so empty anymore. I thought about the directions George had sent, and all the ways he is there for us even when he can't physically be with us.

As a matter of fact, I am sure I saw his figure in the clouds blowing me a kiss until his safe return.

Kim Riley

"Admit it, Mom. You're missing Dad."

Terrorist Brownies

*To love what you do and feel that it matters—
how could anything be more fun?*

Katharine Graham

My husband and I lived in Twentynine Palms, California, until he received orders for an unaccompanied year tour in Okinawa. Housing approved our request to remain, so we stayed in Twentynine Palms while he was away.

I decided to start my own little business of cake-and-goodie baking. I had several connections online through marine support groups, and soon I was baking and delivering cakes to marines stationed here. Shortly after 9/11, I received a call from a mom whose stepson was really stationed at Camp Lejeune in temperate North Carolina, but was out here in the hot desert taking part in a combined-arms exercise. She explained that it was his birthday soon, he loved brownies, and she wanted to do something very special for him. Was there any way I could find him and deliver a birthday treat of brownies to him? she wondered. I said I would try.

After calling several people and being transferred from one office to another, I was finally patched into a field phone and was able to get a message to the marine that he should call me about a birthday surprise. Later that night, he called me and of course was extremely suspicious. He asked me his mother's name, which I of course had to look up. After a mini-interrogation, he agreed to meet at the bowling alley when he had liberty the next day. His mother was unable to reach me that day, so I just went ahead and delivered the brownies, milk, napkins and a homemade card that said, "Love, Mom," to the bowling alley. He had not been able to make it, but his sergeant assured me the marine would get the brownies. Mission accomplished—only better than I had ever imagined.

The next day, I received a phone call from his mother. It seemed this marine finally got his brownies and called his mother at two in the morning. He asked her if she had sent him brownies. She said no, since she was half-asleep. At this point, her son began yelling, "There's been a freaking act of terrorism! You're not going to believe this, but someone sent me poison brownies saying they were from you. And I almost ate them!" He was in an absolute panic.

Then it dawned on her. "Wait, wait," she said, "Are they from an Amie Clark? I was half-asleep when you asked me. I did ask her to find you if she could, but didn't get back to her and had no idea that she found you and delivered the brownies!" They talked for a while longer. He was amazed that she had found him out there.

She later explained to me that their relationship had always been strained, to the point where, if she walked into a room, he would walk out. She had tried several times to reach out to him, but nothing had worked. She told me that the brownies finally opened a door for them. Her gesture made him realize that she loved him, not because she had to but because she wanted to. He now calls the house to talk to her and they sometimes talk for over an hour. The effort she made to send him a birthday treat touched more than his stomach; it touched his soul.

Amie Clark

Destination: Military Wife

I married the first man I ever kissed. When I tell my children that, they just about throw up.

Barbara Bush

When I was in college, my roommate found an address in a magazine where you could send your name and receive the names and addresses of single soldiers who were looking for pen pals. Amy sent in her name, and it wasn't long before her mailbox was crammed with letters from soldiers all over the world. She did her best to reply to each letter she received. One of the soldiers, J. D., was from Rhode Island, just a few miles from where we went to school. He was coming home on leave and wanted to meet her. Amy was nervous, but they hit it off. So well, in fact, that after that weekend, she stopped corresponding with all the other soldiers and focused only on writing to J. D.

A few months after they met, J. D. was deployed to Saudi Arabia in support of Desert Storm. They continued being pen pals for the nine months he was gone. Through their many letters, Amy and J. D. bonded, and their relationship bloomed and deeepened.

The summer J. D. returned home from the Gulf War, Amy and I took a road trip to Fort Bragg, North Carolina, to see him. I was not interested in meeting a soldier, though Amy and J. D. had other plans: they had arranged to set me up with his roommate. Knowing I would protest, they kept it a secret from me until the day before we arrived. That's when J. D.'s roommate had to return home for a death in the family, completely foiling their secret plan. J. D. wanted to find someone else to fill in at the last minute. He told Amy about another squad leader in his platoon, Mitch. Mitch was from Tennessee and wore cowboy boots and liked to sing country music.

Amy leaked this information to me on our way to Fort Bragg. I was understandably upset. First of all, I was embarrassed that they felt they had to fix me up on a blind date. I realized they were doing it so I wouldn't be the third wheel, but it still offended me. Second of all, I am 100 percent Yankee, born in Boston, and I had lived in New England my entire life up until that point. The thought of a "redneck" from Tennessee was not only unappealing, but honestly, quite horrifying. How would I ever relate to a guy who wore cowboy boots and listened to country music? Irritated with my friend despite her good intentions, I told her they could tell Mitch from Tennessee that I weighed five hundred pounds and had unsightly facial hair. They got the point and stopped their scheming.

Amy continued to tease me about "Mitch from Tennessee" for the rest of the drive, and it became a joke to us. When we arrived in Fayetteville, my intentions were to collapse in the hotel room for the remainder of the weekend, only leaving to use the pool. When J. D. showed up at the room twenty minutes after we arrived, they talked me into taking a ride to Fort Bragg for a "quick tour." The last thing I wanted to do was go for a ride, but

Amy's eyes pleaded with me to go.

We saw the sign that welcomed us to Fort Bragg, and our surroundings were immediately transformed. I had never been on an army post before. There were soldiers everywhere. It was intimidating, exciting and interesting. When J. D. pulled into a parking lot and motioned for us to follow him into a building, I glared at Amy. I was haggard and harried from our long journey. "I'm not going anywhere," was what I tried to say. But I knew Amy needed my moral support.

The building we followed J. D. into was the barracks where he lived. As we got close to the door, a guy in army PTs ran past us. When he saw me, he stopped. He was cute and polite and had blood dripping down his forehead from what I later found out was a racquetball accident. He reached his hand out to welcome me to Fort Bragg. "Hi, I'm Mitch," is what he said.

I looked at Amy, and we couldn't contain our laughter. I suddenly wished I had taken a moment to freshen up before we left the hotel room, put on lipstick or at least comb my hair. I knew how bad I looked. Mitch left us to go upstairs, but, a few moments later, he was back, freshly showered and dressed, and following us to J. D.'s truck.

"So where do you want to go eat?" he asked.

I wish I could say we hit it off that night. But, in truth, we did not. I thought he was very attractive and had a great sense of humor. But Mitch was six years older than I, and I found him to be arrogant and overly assertive. Still, we had a fun evening.

When I returned to Rhode Island, I could not stop thinking about him. We started writing, and, after a few more visits to Fort Bragg, our relationship flourished. I graduated from college in May 1993, and I married Mitch from Tennessee in June. We even beat Amy and J. D. to the altar. They said their vows in September of the same year.

As I write this, the year is 2003, and Mitch and I have been happily married for ten years. I know it wasn't luck that led me on that fateful trip to Fort Bragg twelve years ago. It was destiny. We have two beautiful daughters, and Mitch is now a captain with a promising military career ahead of him. He is deployed to the Middle East once again, but this time as a husband and father, rather than a single soldier.

Over the years, I have met many military wives with stories like mine. Nowhere will you find a more diverse group of people than on an army post. We have created a true melting pot in our neighborhoods. I have neighbors from across the globe—from places like Honduras, Korea, Africa, Germany, Vietnam and Croatia. I know wives who met their husbands in bus stations, in airports, in the town squares of foreign countries. There are language barriers, but no barriers stand between our love for our husbands, or the unique friendships we have formed with one another. In the past ten years, a new world has opened up to me. I have been shown that the only race is the human race. I have experienced suffering, and, as a result, I have seen the true strength of the human spirit and the power of support and friendship. There are thousands of military wives, and each one of us has a story to tell about how we got here.

The next time you meet a military wife, take a minute to ask her, "So how did you meet your husband?" It might renew your faith that God has a plan for us all.

Bethany Watkins

Newfound Heroes

No matter what accomplishments you make, somebody helped you.

Althea Gibson

In September 2003 my husband Bill left for Iraq. This deployment was to be different: he was heading to a war zone where our soldiers were being killed and injured. I tried to calm us all by telling the children and myself that he would be okay. He is an excellent soldier and well trained. He was part of a well-trained unit with a good command group. He would be fine. The children were scared, they missed him terribly, but we were managing.

On April 14, 2004, that all changed. The telephone rang, and I heard Bill's voice. He was asking me what I was doing, as if it was any other normal call he had made. Instantly, I could hear in his voice that something was wrong, and asked him if he was okay. He told me that he had been shot, but that everything would be all right. I felt my stomach drop and my blood run cold, one of my worst fears becoming a reality. He had been hit in the left side, the bullet exiting the right side. When he called, he had just arrived at a Baghdad hospital and been stabilized. Some wonderful individual had given him a satellite phone to call his wife. He was able to talk for a few precious moments and then had to go. He was being flown out to Landstuhl Hospital in Germany.

As I hung up the phone, a deep sense of panic set in. I had so many questions that I had not thought to ask while he was on the phone; I didn't know when I would hear from him again and didn't know what to do. I have never felt so helpless in my life. I wanted to be by his side; however, that was not possible. The waiting began.

The next day, there was still no word from him. After an hour of inquiries, transfers and wrong rooms, I was finally connected to his room in Germany. He was doing well, in a lot of pain, but alive. The bullet had missed all major organs. There were shattered bones along the spinal cord, broken ribs and fragments throughout his lower back. It was a bad injury, but he was still miraculously able to walk. At that moment, I realized how blessed we were, how miraculous it was that he was able to talk to me at all on the phone.

He arrived home on April 21. The doctors told us that this was going to be a very long recovery, but that they were optimistic he would make a full recovery. They also told us how incredibly lucky we were that he was in this condition. The fact that the bullet missed any vital organs was an absolute miracle, and we counted ourselves extremely lucky.

My husband has always been a hero to me, but even more so now—he came home to me. I also found a new set of heroes that day: the soldiers who fought beside him, saving his life. The soldier who lost his own life in that battle. The others who were wounded beside him. The wonderful man who pulled my husband to safety amidst a barrage of bullets. The medic who worked on him, keeping him alive until help could arrive. And the medical personnel who evacuated him and kept him alive until he could be treated. All these people were heroes to me before, in spirit; however, after this day, they became so in reality. I will never meet them all, will never know most of the men who helped to save his life, but they are my heroes all the same.

Carol Howard

The Angel at the Olive Garden

We differ from others only in what we do and don't do, not in what we are.

Anthony DeMello

My husband was deployed in February 2003 to serve in Operation Iraqi Freedom. One Friday night after he had been gone for several months, my son and I joined my father for dinner at the Olive Garden. My son, who is a year old, is quite the entertainer, and he began engaging the waitress as soon as she came over to the table. After speaking with him for a while, she told me that he looked just like his dad. She assumed my father was my son's father. I explained that his dad was in Iraq and that the man at the table was his grandfather. She told me that she would keep my husband and me in her prayers.

After a while, our dinner was served. We were enjoying ourselves at the table when a man walked up to the table and said, "Did I hear you say that your husband was in Iraq?"

I replied, "Yes, he is."

He asked me if my husband was in the military, and I once again replied in the affirmative. The man then handed me a hundred-dollar bill, telling me to do him a favor and have dinner on him and buy my son something with whatever was left over. My eyes welled up with tears, and the man just walked away. I asked my father to follow him and get his name so that I could thank him. My dad went outside and followed the man to his car and asked for his name, but this lovely stranger refused to give my father any information. All he would say was that it made him sad to see a young mother and her son out while her husband was fighting a war.

Diane L. Flowers

You Didn't Tell Me

You told me about the long shifts, the days and nights.
You told me about the commanders and their lovely wives.
You told me about chain of command, and how I would
    live by it.
But you didn't tell me how proud of you I would be.
You told me about the temporary duty and the many moves.
You told me about overseas tours.
You told me about payday, and how we would stretch the
    dollar.
You didn't tell me about the honor I would feel.
You told me about the wives' clubs and family support.
You told me about Tricare.
You told me about base housing, and how no two are alike.
You didn't tell me that at the start of "God Bless the USA"
    I would shed not one, but many tears.
You told me about how Christmas would be in Germany.
You told me about the commissary and PX.
You told me we would need many sets of curtains.
You didn't tell me how our children would look up to you,
    and want to be like Dad.
You told me about the hard times and how we would have
    many.

You told me about the stress of being a military spouse.

You told me sometimes I would be a single parent, and that in spirit you would be with me.

But you didn't tell me that when I saw your uniform in the laundry, I would swell with respect.

You didn't tell me how much of a part the military would play in our lives and how I would never want it any other way!

Donna Porter

Hooah

*We ordinary people must forge our own beauty.
We must set fire to the grayness of our labor with
the art of our own lives.*

Kenji Meyazawa

When I found out the news of Larry's deployment, I quickly realized that I'd be in a new city alone, in a new job, in a new house, without many new friends, no children of our own and no family living close by. I had no idea who or what would surface to keep me going and support me through the time he'd be away. I just had to trust that they would appear.

And appear they did: in the form of a small group of seventh-grade mothers and the entire cast of two hundred students at Sacred Heart Middle School where I'm a teacher.

In September, just prior to his deployment, my husband visited my students. Captain Larry, as the students called him, gave an outstanding PowerPoint presentation (worthy of an A+). He showed them maps of Kosovo, teaching them about the peacekeeping mission he'd be a part of, and, of course, the many possible meanings of the word "Hooah!" They were mesmerized to see a soldier up close.

One cool October night at a parent/teacher conference, my seventh-grade student, John, asked me, "Mrs. Doss, when does your husband get home?"

"Sometime next September, I think, but we can't be sure," I replied.

When John's mom overheard his question on that autumn evening, she asked, "Mrs. Doss, what do you mean? Where is your husband?"

Realizing that John hadn't told his parents about Larry, I proceeded to tell her that he was deployed to Kosovo with the Iowa National Guard, and would be gone for the next year.

Her questions came like a flood: "Do you have children? Do you own a home? Do you have family nearby? Do you have a pet?" Her outpouring of care and concern for me was heartwarming. But there was no way I could have been prepared for what was to come.

A letter was sent home to the middle-school parents, stating that there would be an "Out of Uniform Day" for all students donating one dollar or more. In a private school, the students value these opportunities to sport their latest fashion purchases. That being said, I was expecting our two hundred students to raise about a hundred dollars or so.

You can imagine my surprise when those same two hundred students brought in about eight hundred dollars on the Out of Uniform Day. With a little help from the student council, the students and their mothers used a thousand dollars to purchase two-hour phone cards and prayer cards for each of the 180 soldiers in my husband's unit.

The same group of mothers declared April 1 to be "Mrs. Doss's Day." My room was decorated for the likes of a military ball, and my corsage made me feel like the belle of the ball. The patriotic stars and stripes spilled out into the hallway and dribbled on every other classroom door in the place. Matching decorations were carefully packed in the box headed for Kosovo so that my husband and his unit could decorate along with us. There was a huge banner that the students signed, sending their love, prayers, support and gratitude to the soldiers protecting their freedom and their safety.

There were so many other surprises for me throughout the year, including a Valentine's Day gift, an Easter basket (signed "From the Easter Bunny," of course), as well as two huge welcome-home baskets of goodies to use in celebrating my husband's return. One student brought a bag of HERSHEY'S KISSES to comfort me while my husband was away, and another presented me with a stuffed dog that looked exactly like my own Boston terrier, Toby. She thought having a stuffed Toby at school would keep me from getting lonely. There were lots of questions about how I was doing, who was shoveling my driveway, how the house was holding up and an occasional "Hooah" when the kids thought it appropriate. It always made me laugh, no matter what I was trying to teach!

Before my husband's deployment, I envisioned "serving your country" as serving in the armed forces and a few other choice careers that also fit the bill. Now, I know that serving your country involves so much more.

When we help each other in times of need, when we volunteer our time and effort to make our schools and cities better places, we serve our country. When we become informed voters and concerned citizens, we serve our country. When we support the families and friends of deployed soldiers, we serve our country. Good deeds strengthen our communities, and, one by one, they build a strong nation. This is what "united we stand" is all about.

I hope and pray that my students learned a lot about reading and language arts from me this year. I trust they learned the true meaning of patriotism as well. Hooah!

Theresa Doss

8

AN OFFICER AT THE DOOR

What we have once enjoyed, we can never lose. All that we love deeply becomes a part of us.

Helen Keller

His Name Was John

What do we live for, if not to make life less dif-
ficult for each other?

George Eliot

In the airline industry, there is no such thing as a routine day. Anything can happen. Today, it was a mechanical
problem with the aircraft. Until a mechanic came on
board, we were to remain in the airplane and wait for final
word about our departure. Of course, the passengers
were not happy about the news.

I was talking with the other flight attendants when I
felt a tap on my shoulder. A young woman, perhaps
twenty-five years old, was standing before me.

"May I talk to you?" she whispered quietly.

"Of course," I said to her as I took her arm to sit with her
in the empty seats in row one. The look in her eyes told me
something was wrong.

"I'm Andrea," she began. "I'm flying with two friends.
We're Marine Corps wives. My friend, Joanna, is asleep by
the window. We're flying to Denver and then on to New
York today. See, Joanna's husband was killed in Iraq on

Wednesday, and we're going to his funeral. We just *have* to get there today.

"We've given her two sleeping pills," she continued. "We thought we'd be in the air for a couple of hours, and she needs to sleep. They got married just a year ago on Valentine's Day. John and Joanna were the perfect couple. John was gone just two months on his first tour of duty. That's his Marine Corps sweatshirt she's wearing to comfort her."

My heart sank. My mind raced. *These girls are going to miss their connections to New York. What can I do?* I thought to myself. Out loud, all I said was, "I'm so sorry. Let me see what I can do."

Nobody was supposed to leave the aircraft, but I asked the captain if I might take the tickets of these three passengers to the gate agent to see if there was something that could be done. Nearly half the passengers had connecting flights, but, when the gate agent heard the story, she set out to get them on another plane.

When I returned to the airplane, I could see Andrea talking to the now-awake Joanna. Her hands held her face as she sobbed. I leaned over the two friends and touched Joanna for the first time. Again, all I could say was, "I'm so sorry."

The wait was becoming longer and longer. People were getting antsy. I went to row four and said to Joanna, "Come with me." I took her hand and led her to the front of the aircraft, behind the bulkhead, near the door. I just put my arm around her and held her. She cried. I cried. She held a rosary in her hand, but Andrea had said she was really mad at God right now. I understood. We just stood there, the two of us.

Finally, the gate agent came on board. She'd pulled some strings, made some phone calls and somehow managed to get all three women a direct flight from California to New York. I left Joanna for a moment, got her two friends and all their carry-on items. We deplaned. I'm sure the other passengers wondered why they were allowed off the aircraft. There would be time for explanations later.

I hugged all three women, took a deep breath, wiped the tears from my eyes and went back to the plane.

God, take care of them, I offered before heading back to work. Joanna's two friends were there for her, just like she'd be there for them if the dice had rolled differently. They were *all* military wives.

They *did* leave that airport. They flew on a direct flight to New York City. I learned that they would be met by a military limo and taken to John's parents' home in New Jersey. I never talked with them again. I probably never will. But, today, my thoughts are with them. It was a hard day for Joanna. Fortunately, she had her friends to support her as she said her good-bye, one last time, to her young husband, John.

I wish I'd had the honor of meeting John. I know I'll never forget Joanna.

Mary Catherine Carwile

Anticipation

Spirit is an invisible force made visible in all life.

Maya Angelou

It didn't matter that rain droplets were falling, dampening my dress and hair.

I was in Hawaii. It was June 1968. The palm fronds danced, touched by the raindrops and the breeze, and my heart danced, too. I was waiting for my young husband— the love of my life—to alight from the bus to begin his R&R (rest and recuperation) from Vietnam.

The plan had been for a group of us to go to the Processing Center to intercept Denny, my in-laws' only son. Pap, a former military officer, had figured out how to circumvent the military's guideline that soldiers take cabs from the drop-off location to where their families were staying.

It was strange, but as we dressed that morning to leave the hotel, I felt glum. I wondered about it. Since Denny left for Vietnam, I had waited for this day, for the opportunity to be with him and hold him tight. And yet there I was—eager but also quiet, withdrawn, anxious. What was bothering me?

My mother-in-law, in her kind way, understood what I did not. "Honey," she asked, "would you like to meet Denny yourself at the Processing Center, and we'll wait here at the hotel?"

My father-in-law was outraged at her suggestion. "No! Of course not," he exclaimed. "We're all going together!"

She urged him gently. "Let her go herself. They're a married couple now. We'll see them when they get back to the hotel."

It was yet another kindness when my father-in-law acquiesced to his wife's suggestion. When I realized I would be going alone to the Processing Center, my spirits rose, and I felt happy, even elated.

Off I went, too early, really. I dutifully stood near a sign that stated: Family Members, This Area Only. Obviously, they anticipated that others would find out where the men would arrive.

Then came a third kind gesture, this time from a stranger. A workman approached and asked if I was waiting for the bus arriving from the airport.

"Yes, I am," I replied. The workman left.

Twenty minutes later, he returned.

"The plane has just arrived," he told me. "After they board the bus, they'll be here in about thirty minutes." I felt my stomach jump at his words.

"Thank you," I said shyly.

"And," he continued, "if you follow me over here, this is *right where* the bus will unload." He gestured and started moving to another side of the building and then saw my hesitation. "It's okay; come wait over here," he said.

Even with the rain, I was not about to leave my specially assigned post. Looking down, I saw that my colorful flower lei was bleeding purple onto the white yoke of my sundress. But no matter. As I continued to wait, I was lost in my thoughts, feeling quiet and withdrawn once again.

Denny and I began dating in college; his senior year, my sophomore year. A year later, as the Vietnam War activity increased, he enlisted in the marines.

When it became apparent he would likely be sent to 'Nam, we decided to marry in March. We lived together in Quantico, Virginia, as he completed officer's training. Denny was the first love of my life, and we treasured our six months together before he departed in September. During our eight-month separation, I pored eagerly over the letters I received from him. They were usually smudged with dirt and mud; he was experiencing heavy combat. I wrote him nearly every day.

But now I was afraid—fearful that I wouldn't recognize this husband of mine. At home, I would look often at the photo of Denny posing in his military uniform and study the image again and again. I would search my memory for the moments we shared together, and hear his laughter, see his blue eyes, his broad shoulders, his smile. But this day I was fearful that perhaps I wouldn't recognize the man I had chosen to marry and who was now a marine second lieutenant. I drew in my breath and felt anxiety rise inside me once again as not one, but three, buses stopped in front of me, one behind the other. The workman had been correct: the buses would unload directly in front of where I was standing.

My trepidation grew as, one by one, soldiers stepped down from each bus and began walking quietly past me into the Processing Center, where they would be debriefed and sent to meet their families.

I didn't see Denny. As the soldiers continued to walk past me, I became afraid. What if Denny came down the bus steps and I was standing there empty of recognition, staring at but not seeing that the man in front of me is my precious husband? How will I find the face I so long to see, the face in the photograph?

And then he was there. The split second of recognition was so powerful, it swept through my entire body and being. And all it took was seeing a pair of boots and pant legs to the knees, waiting to descend the steps. I knew it was Denny—his stance, his legs, his feet in boots.

In that instant, I flew through the empty space between us, colliding with him as his first boot touched the ground. I hugged him, overcome by his presence and the realization that we were together again. Denny grinned and embraced me.

What was it that made me so powerfully aware of his presence? It was not his photograph or even the memories of our relationship that enabled me to recognize him.

What I learned that day is that the most powerful bonds we share with those we love deeply and everlastingly are not rooted in the physical. More than smiles, mannerisms and voices, we come to know the spiritual part of one another.

Denny's very essence communicated to me that day in Hawaii. Denny's spirit and his love shouted to me from the top of those bus steps. My recognition happened in an instant so fast I can't describe it, and it happened because of the love that connected us.

Denny didn't come home from Vietnam, and I have replayed in my mind many, many times the last days we shared in this world. And I know that, in the imperceptible dimension where love resides, Denny and I remain connected forever.

Judith Hodge Andrews Dennis
As told to Marjorie Kramer

Accepting the Folded Flag

The love of our neighbor in all its fullness sim-
ply means being able to say, "What are you going
through?"

Simone Weil

I have watched them fold the flag more times than I can
remember. The first time, I stood stiffly, noticing the
mechanical movements of the navy honor guardsmen
flanking the grave site as they lifted the flag from the casket and began to fold it into a tight triangle. Their practiced, white-gloved hands moved quickly to manipulate
the fabric and smooth potential wrinkles, passing the
thickening shape down the line of men, until all I could
see were the bright white stars on the blue background.
The men were meticulous with their movements, careful
not to let the sacred banner touch the ground. The leader
of the guard stepped forward to accept the finished triangle from the two men who gripped it so somberly at the
end of the lines. He inspected the angles and tucked the
loose end under the last fold to secure it. Then he walked
slowly to face the petite woman shrouded in symbolic black.

Nelly, my dearest friend, stood stiffly, shoulders taut with the weight of the occasion, but her chin held high. Her eyes were swollen and dark from a week of sleepless nights and endless crying. With her long hair hanging loose, she looked beautiful in spite of her overwhelming sadness, radiating strength for her young sons, who stood on either side of her.

As the guardsman approached, she squeezed the two hands held in her own and then let them drop out of her grasp to accept the flag offered to her. Her eyes met mine for a moment, and a current passed between us. Neither of us could believe that this husband, father, best friend, lover and hero had been reduced to a folded flag. Her hands shook. I wanted to reach out and take the flag for her, to share her pain so that she would not have to bear it alone. She looked down at the flag and buried her face in the fabric, weeping softly but openly.

"Mama?" whimpered three-year-old Chris, pulling at his mother's arm in confusion. Nelly's sister immediately scooped up the child and rocked him gently from side to side while whispering softly in his ear. Benjamin, who was five and understood more than his little brother, leaned against his mother and began to cry.

We stood at attention as a bugler on a distant hill began to play the lonesome strains of "Taps." I could not pull my eyes away from mother and children. Both the boys flinched and Chris began to cry when the riflemen on the opposite hill raised their guns and fired. Three rounds of seven shots invaded the silence in the customary twenty-one-gun salute to the honor of a fallen warrior. As the last notes of the bugle echoed in the air and the smoke drifted into the blue afternoon sky, feelings of sadness and pride settled over the crowd gathered at the grave site.

The sound of aircraft engines filled the air. A hush fell over the crowd. All eyes scanned the sky for the planes we knew would arrive momentarily. The four A-6 Intruders, flying in the shape of an arrowhead, moved in to fly over the crowd and grave site below. When they were directly overhead, the jet positioned slightly back and right of the lead broke formation and flew up and away from the group, disappearing deep into the heavens. The remaining three jets flew over our heads in the symbolic "missing man" formation, leaving the gap between them open. It was a maneuver used only as a salute to fallen aviators. Yet another hero had gone.

This was the first of many families I would stand with at Arlington National Cemetery. Through almost nineteen years as a naval aviator's wife, I have watched widows, children, parents and siblings reluctantly reach out to accept that folded symbol of our nation's honor and service. I have seen a young wife collapse in sobs, a confused toddler salute the bugler and a teenager march somberly behind a horse and carriage carrying the flag-draped casket of his dad, his greatest hero.

Out of that overwhelming despair, new heroes have arisen. Unsung by politicians, newspapers and medals of honor, Nelly and others like her have steeled their emotions and mustered their courage to face the future. They have protected the memory and honor of that symbolic flag, and passed it on to their children in spite of lonely days, sleepless nights and painful insensitivities from the world around them. They have emerged from their grief to provide homes full of love, joy and security for their children, a testament to the power of God and the human spirit.

For all those who have accepted the folded flag, I thank you for your sacrifice. I thank you for demonstrating daily acts of heroism that few appreciate or even recognize. You are a gentle reminder that, though the sun may sometimes set with glorious colors, plunging the world into darkness, the hope of a new and brilliant dawn is just beyond the horizon.

Saundra L. Butts

A Widow's Salvation

*The shadows of the evening run deep while love
comes in to soothe every mind and body.*

Kabir

Catalina's husband had been in Vietnam for almost a
year. In the beginning, he had written to her faithfully—
she would get a letter from him once a week. But the letters had stopped coming, and it had been nine long
weeks since Catalina had heard from him. At home,
Catalina was doing her best to keep the faith and manage
the household of five young children on a small budget.
Her hands were full, and her mind was worried.

Catalina had been married to Floyd Dean Caldwell for
sixteen years, all of which he had devoted to the military. Raised in extreme poverty in Mexico, she met her
husband-to-be while he was stationed in a border town
in Texas, where she would cross the border to attend
adult-education classes. They were a military family,
and Catalina knew that the U.S. Army had been her salvation. The military had provided the means for them to
feed, clothe and house their five young children.

It was their military lifestyle and benefits, while not extravagant, that had allowed them to get the medical attention they needed when Catalina was diagnosed with tuberculosis shortly after they married, and when their daughter was born prematurely with severe asthma. Military life had not only allowed them to support their family, but also to live in parts of the world that they might never have seen otherwise. Catalina had a great appreciation for all the ways in which her life and her family's life had been blessed by her husband's military duty.

When Floyd was sent to Vietnam, she prayed for continued blessings.

Then his letters stopped. After nine weeks of worrying and waiting, she contacted the Red Cross. In her broken English, she told the Red Cross representative about her concerns. The Red Cross contacted the U.S. Army, and an investigation was immediately begun as to his whereabouts. As if he had a premonition that something might happen to him, Floyd had left all his military papers in an envelope for Catalina to use in case of an emergency. These papers began the investigation that would reveal the unthinkable.

It was discovered that Floyd Dean Caldwell had boarded a U-21 aircraft in Phu Bai Airfield in South Vietnam on December 14, 1971. He had gotten his orders to go home and had hopped an early flight with hopes of getting to his family as soon as possible. He was not scheduled to board that plane, but an officer in front of him in line had said, "Go ahead, take my place; you have a family to get home to. I'll take the next one." That fateful generosity placed my father, Floyd Dean Caldwell, on the flight to his death. The plane's twin engines caught fire, and the aircraft exploded in flames over the South China Sea. No remains were ever found.

When the two uniformed officers approached Catalina's home to inform her of her husband's death, her mind was racing. Her house was filled with the energetic activity of her children and their friends playing, doing homework, reading—being children. Chaos filled her home and her thoughts as she tried to listen to the officers tell her the findings of the investigation. She wondered how she would survive, how—with no education or training beyond a high-school diploma from Mexico—she would provide for her five children.

She wondered how she would tell her children that their father would not be coming home for Christmas that year—or any year . . . that he was with God now. She bit back her tears as she began to gather what strength she could to get through this moment to the next.

As it turned out, Catalina and her family continued to be blessed by her husband's military duty, even after his death. The U.S. Army took care of a family of a soldier lost in a war, making sure that my mother was able to move forward with her life and support her children. She was able to place a down payment on a modest house and go back to school. Catalina earned not only her bachelor's degree, but also her master's in education, all while working full-time as a teacher and teaching adult-education classes in the evenings. In 1981, my mother received an award for Outstanding Teaching and Learning in Education in recognition of all her hard work and accomplishments.

Thanks to the assistance given by the army, each of her five children had the opportunity to attend college. Her two sons chose to follow in their father's footsteps, and were commissioned as officers in the U.S. Army when they completed college. They served their country just as their father had done. Her youngest son is presently a major in the Texas National Guard.

All this was made possible by the life and death of my father, SSgt. Floyd Dean Caldwell, and his service to our country. Catalina says prayers of gratitude each night for how her husband's life was not given in vain. During his life, he served in a war fought for freedom and democracy. His death enabled his wife and family to be taken care of in ways that Catalina would never have dreamed of. When my mother, Catalina Caldwell, speaks with reverence and gratitude about the life that her husband gave in service to this country, she never fails to mention the ways this country gave back to her and her family.

Lora Vivas

A Little Thing

$W\!e$ *can know the dark and dream it into a*
new image.

Starhawk

[EDITORS' NOTE: *The following reaction to the news of*
Canadian casualties in Afghanistan was written for CBC News
Online by Jodi Chappel, the wife of a member of the Canadian
Forces based in Winnipeg.]

My name is Jodi. I'm a thirty-two-year-old mother of
two—Roman, twelve and Phoenix, seven—and my husband is a navigator on the C–130 Hercules at 435 squadron
in Winnipeg. He is currently on standby to be one of the
next crews to rotate into Afghanistan. In light of what has
happened in the last few days, this scares me to death.

As I walked home from work today past the gates of the
base I could see the somber reminders of the events of the
last few days. The flag is at half-mast and there is already
a sea of white ribbons in support of the families that have
lost loved ones.

Last night, I turned on the television to check the
weather before I went to bed. According to breaking news

reports, four Canadians had been killed and eight others wounded by friendly fire in Afghanistan. I watched with utter disbelief. A lump swelled in my throat. The tears welled up in my eyes and I felt a wave of panic.

As I'm sure every other military family in Canada did as they heard the news, I started going through the list in my mind of all our friends and neighbors who were over there. Thinking *oh my God what if it was* . . . then the phone started to ring. It was my girlfriend and neighbor asking me if I had heard the news. She asked if I had heard who it was or which company they were from. She sounded frantic. I told her that I didn't know and suggested that she call the base in case they knew. I tried my hardest to reassure her that it wasn't her husband, pointing out that if it were she would have heard by now, telling her that he was fine and would soon be calling her to let her know he was all right.

On the couch, I choked back tears and thought about the poor wives and families who would be awoken by a knock on the door. That knock on the door, men in dress uniforms and the military padre on the porch, is the thing that we fear most, and my heart goes out to the families that had to experience that last night.

Military families are taught this might someday happen but I don't think we are ever quite prepared. We learn to function alone for very long periods of time, adjusting to our loved one's absences but comforted by the expectation of their return.

Losing four members of a very close-knit community has shaken us all to the core. As a military wife, my heart goes out to families that have lost loved ones, and the families of the ones who are hurt. As a Canadian, a human being and a mother, I pray for an end to war, in every form.

It takes a strong person to love a member of the military because of the things we have to give up. But we gain something much greater: that overwhelming sense of pride that comes with choosing to live in ways that serve our country. The military is a family. We depend and rely on each other, and in an hour of need we share the strength, comfort and understanding that only a family member can understand. We know the hardships of being lonely. We have also waited by the phone once a week to hear a particular voice tell us that they are alright, and that they miss us.

I have a little thing I make my husband do before he goes away for any length of time. I make him sing to me on tape and tell me and the children he loves us. If anything should ever happen to him, we will always have that. Because that's what I would miss the most. A soft "I love you, Jodi; I love you, Roman, I love you, Phoenix" and him singing "Unchained Melody" by the Righteous Brothers. In our own way we all make preparations. We just pray that day will never arrive.

Jodi Chappel

Somebody Knew Gene

Pray for the dead and fight like hell for the living.

Mother Mary Jones

A bright swath of cloudless blue sky arched over the road that morning. The radio news broadcast reported that an American soldier died in an ambush during a search for Al Qaeda and Taliban fighters in the mountains of eastern Afghanistan. I felt a sadness, a sort of distant and muted grief. I felt it every time I heard of a death of one of our soldiers.

"What did he say, Mom?" my five-year-old daughter, Lauren, asked from the backseat.

I quickly ran through various explanations in my mind. Although I tried to shelter my kids from as much violence and evil as I could, it seemed the simple truth was the best choice in this situation.

"He said a soldier died fighting the bad people." I'd tried to make the complex issues of terrorism understandable with simple, clear-cut terms.

"What's a soldier?"

"A person in the military," I said.

"Like Dad?"

"Yes, like Dad, but it didn't have anything to do with Dad." I tried to reassure her. "We didn't know the person." Since my husband is in the Air Force Reserve we'd talked about Dad doing his job as a pilot to help fight the bad people. I didn't want Lauren to worry about her dad being hurt or killed.

"What was his name?" she asked.

"Who?"

"The man who died," she persisted. "What was his name?"

"It was Gene, honey, but we didn't know him. You don't need to worry."

"But somebody knew Gene." I knew from the tone of her voice, the echo of my own sorrow I heard there, that she understood what had happened. I glanced back and saw her eyes glazed with tears.

The brilliant sky and the tender new leaves misting the trees blurred together with the blackness of the road. I signaled to turn into the school parking lot and fought the tightness in my throat. "I know. Gene had a family and friends," I managed to say. "Should we say a prayer for them?"

Lauren nodded, and I managed to choke out a simple prayer for comfort.

I deposited Lauren and her brother in their classrooms, and they dove into the day's activities, the bleak news forgotten. But I didn't forget. Lauren's simple statement, "Somebody knew Gene," has stayed with me. What an eloquent yet straightforward reminder of the sacrifice of military members and their families. Time passes, and the families and friends might think the sacrifice has been forgotten. But it hasn't been. I still think of Gene.

So, to Gene's family, to Antonio's family, to Christopher's family, to Anissa's family, to John's family, to Nathan's family, to Evander's family, to Stanley's family and to so many countless other families who grieve for a loved one, know that we pray for your comfort, we are awed by the sacrifice of your son, daughter, husband, wife or friend— but, above all, know we are grateful.

Sara Rosett

The Christmas Tree

How wonderful it is that nobody need wait a single moment before starting to improve the world.

Anne Frank

Christmas 1970 was going to be a very special holiday, even though my husband, Joe, was away. My entire immediate family was going to be at Mom's house. I was so happy to be a part of the celebrations that year; with my husband in Vietnam and me expecting a baby any day, the best place for me and my two-year-old, Melanie, was at home. My two brothers, Mom, Dad, Melanie and I would all be together.

Even though Joe couldn't be there, I knew that his job as an army intelligence officer was very important to him. He was happy to be able to serve his country, even though he was doing it on the other side of the world.

When I was a child, the Christmas tree was always the most fun to decorate. Dad would chop down a tree from our property, and no matter how oddly it might be shaped, we would decorate it with love. This year, Dad went out and bought a beautiful tree, fresh and perfectly shaped. It was standing proudly in the corner, bare and green, while Mom and I cleaned up in preparation for our big Italian family.

Neither one of us heard the knock at the door. Suddenly, my sister-in-law and two handsome men dressed in full army uniforms appeared before me. They introduced themselves as casualty-assistance officers. The news was the worst a young wife could receive: Joe had been killed on December 16 in a helicopter that crashed and burned. My world was shattered at that moment.

After the officers left, Mom and I knew that we had to cancel Christmas. The first thing that went was our beautiful Christmas tree. There are many foggy memories of that first horrible day, but the image of our Christmas tree being dragged out of the house is still vivid in my mind. Little Melanie couldn't understand why so many of us were crying.

Early on Christmas Eve morning, I gave birth to my second child, Josette. Later that morning, my husband was buried. My family was emotionally exhausted, and I didn't know what was going on, as I was still sedated from the birth. Since I was in the hospital for Christmas Eve, Mom, Dad and my brothers took care of Melanie.

On Christmas Eve, my brothers brought out all the gifts from Santa Claus, but there was no tree. My brother Charles, a forester from the state of Washington, told the other family members that Melanie couldn't go through Christmas without a tree, so he went out late at night and chopped down a short, skinny "Charlie Brown" tree that could hardly hold any ornaments. They decorated it as best they could. On Christmas morning, Melanie woke up to see all her gifts under the little tree. As in most Italian families—and especially because of the circumstances—relatives came to visit, and Melanie was the center of attention.

Melanie was excited about the toys and gifts, but the most fascinating thing for her on that Christmas morning was being surprised by the "beautifully" decorated little tree. When everyone asked Melanie what she had gotten for Christmas, she proudly announced that Santa Claus had given her a Christmas tree.

That tree helped make Christmas wonderful for a little girl who had just lost her daddy.

Joanne Danna

A Bittersweet Photograph

I sat in the dark family room of the neonatal ICU in Camp Lester, holding hands with my husband, Erik, and shaking. I couldn't do this, not now, not ever. I was about to hold my baby for the first time, and for the last. The room seemed to grow darker, and I felt like I was living in a horrible dream.

My twin sons Keegan and Tristan were born three months prematurely at a naval hospital on Okinawa. They both had been fighting an incredible battle, while the team of military doctors and nurses did all they could. But Tristan's lungs were too premature, and he was dying.

On the tenth day, Erik and I watched and waited, knowing in our hearts that the whisper of God's calling was more powerful than any drug or procedure on the planet. Although my heart understood, my mind couldn't wrap around the fact that I would no longer be able to hold, smell, kiss, sing to or see my son. Then a woman I had only seen in passing, Capt. Karen Larry, stepped into the room.

Capt. Larry looked us each in the eye and placed her healing hands over both of ours. "I don't know if the two of you have thought about this," she said gently, "but with your permission, I would like to take some photographs of Tristan for you."

I had heard of parents taking photos with stillborn children, but I wasn't sure. Capt. Larry could see the doubt in my face. "I also lost a baby," she told us. "Some parents have found it a comfort to have a photograph. It can be for just the two of you." A tiny candle took flame in a pitch-black room. Through my tears, I agreed, and then Erik did, too.

When the nurse brought Tristan in, my husband and I began to sob. It was the first time we had seen him without wires or tubes connected to him. There were no whirring machines drowning out his tiny breathing. He was all wrapped up in a soft blanket and a little soft beanie hat, and he finally looked like a baby. Like our baby. While my husband and I held Tristan for the first and last time, Capt. Larry quietly began taking photographs. I was so overwhelmed by emotions that, had she not asked our permission, I probably would not have noticed her. As soon as we took comfort in the moment, Tristan took a final labored breath, and then he was gone.

The next few days were an emotionally exhausting haze. My other son Keegan was doing much better, but my heart was still shattered by Tristan's death. Once again, Capt. Larry brought light into my day. She gave me a package, and, when Erik came home, we opened it together.

Capt. Larry had created a treasure for us. Not only were there photos of us holding our precious son, but she also had taken the extra time to photograph him after he had passed. He looked so peaceful, bundled up and lying next to the teddy bear that my mother had gotten for him the day the twins were born. There was so much in this black-and-white photograph that was familiar. Tristan's nose, his face and his little hands were just like mine. His little body had been so consumed by all the wires that I had not truly seen the resemblance until just that moment. With her camera, Capt. Larry had captured a true feeling of peace, something any mother would wish for her firstborn son. I hugged the photos and Erik, while we both cried.

More than a month later, I was allowed to spend my first night alone in the postpartum ward with Keegan. Capt. Larry, who had become a dear friend during our stay in the NICU, came to visit and take Keegan's vitals, and I told her how much she meant to our family and how precious was the gift she had given to us. Tears had become a regular part of our conversations, for they flowed sometimes without reason when we were together. We found a common ground in our quest for motherhood, and in the losses and triumphs of the lives we had created.

We returned to the States, and my dear friend Capt. Larry remains a part of our lives. We have shared many e-mails and photographs, but that one bittersweet image is still the centerpiece of our bound lives. This dear, simple act of kindness touches me every day. The black-and-white photo that Capt. Larry took is in Keegan's room, and I take comfort in knowing that Tristan watches over his little brother.

We have many pictures of family and friends hanging on our walls, but one stands out. It is a black-and-white photograph of Capt. Larry, with tears in her eyes and love in her heart. She is holding Keegan.

Amy Naegeli

A Family Like No Other

After growing up an air force brat, I knew about moving into a new home every three years, starting new schools in strange places, and making new friends only to leave them behind. I vowed never to marry into the military.

Six months after marrying A1C Mark Norris, the air force moved us from family, friends and safety to the unknown wilds of Alaska. We were together on the honeymoon of a lifetime.

I missed my family, but we soon grew to depend on another military couple, Kevin and Amy. It was nice having friends to celebrate holidays with, to do errands for you while you were ill, or even to shovel your driveway when your husband was stationed in another part of the world.

After Amy gave birth to twin boys, Mark and I decided to have a baby. Getting pregnant wasn't easy, but after a round of fertility drugs, we finally saw that pink plus sign on the pregnancy test!

I couldn't wait to call our families! The next call was to Amy, followed by more talks through the weeks, as every little twitch required Amy's pregnancy expertise. She always reassured me that everything I was experiencing was normal, until one night I started spotting. I went to the hospital, where I was given an ultrasound. The doctor smiled at me. "How do you feel about twins?"

We were anxious to tell everyone we were having twins. I was sure my pregnancy would be easy, just as Amy's had been. However, that wasn't the case. Almost immediately, all-day sickness set in. I lost a lot of weight and went on bed rest at twenty weeks gestation.

The military was wonderful to Mark during this time, allowing him to take me to my doctor's appointments. Our military friends were just as great. They would drop by to visit. Some would bring dinner. Amy brought me information on multiple births and raising twins.

One night, while Mark was involved in a military exercise, I felt a gush of liquid. I knew that thirty weeks was too early, and called Mark's squadron in tears. He met me at the Elmendorf Air Force Base hospital emergency room, and, the next morning, I was ambulanced to Providence Hospital, a better-equipped facility for premature deliveries.

Even as the neonatologist explained the risks to us, I was sure that things would be fine. As an unfamiliar doctor was talking about an emergency cesarean section, I went into a fog. My mother wasn't there! Nothing was as I had planned, except having Mark by my side.

Our babies were born at noon in a cold, sanitary operating room filled with a dozen or so strangers there to save their lives. I didn't get to see my babies, hear them cry or hold them before their tiny bodies were rushed through a window into the neonatal ICU. After waking up from the surgery, I was wheeled into a room where Hailey and Zachary had bright lights beaming down on them, while tubes and wires attached every part of their wrinkled bodies to lifesaving devices.

As I looked up, a skylight revealed the first snow of the season. It was so beautiful, so pure. I was filled with love and fear. Through an open window, we could see a statue of a saint holding a small boy in his arms. For me, the view was symbolic. It meant that my babies were held in the arms of the protector. Our prayers together began that instant, with Mark uttering words meant only for God and myself.

As soon as she heard that I had given birth, Amy appeared with helium-filled balloons that proclaimed, "It's a girl!" and "It's a boy!" This lifted my spirits as I drifted to sleep.

The following morning I noticed that Zachary's balloon had fallen slightly lower than Hailey's. A nurse from NICU rushed in, taking us to a neonatologist standing beside Zachary. Things weren't going well. By dinner-time, the balloon had nearly fallen to the floor. We were summoned back to the NICU for a last chance to say good-bye to our son.

Zachary died in Mark's arms, just after being told it was okay to go to heaven.

During the night, the news had traveled through our circle of friends and up the chain of command. A military chaplain was with us for support. He arranged to have the Red Cross fly our parents up, and even guided us through funeral arrangements. Mark's squadron commander came by, telling him not to worry about returning to work but to take care of his family first. The Airmen's Emergency Fund provided funds for the funeral.

I can never repay our military family for the love and support they gave us during our time of loss. Mark's bud-dies from work were granted permission to leave duty to console Mark, and Amy came to me. While our relatives were on their way, our military family provided the immediate comfort we needed. Amy even went to our house, returning the double items meant for Zachary, so we wouldn't have to face them on our first night home.

We received orders to move to McConnell Air Force Base in Wichita, Kansas. Hailey remained in the hospital growing stronger, and came home on her actual due date, December 16. By the end of February, we were packing up for our move. Our Alaskan military family saw us off at the airport, as we took off to build our family in Kansas.

Before we left, I looked over to the corner of Hailey's room. There it was, her balloon, still fully inflated and floating over her crib as she napped peacefully.

Ann Hail Norris

War—A Widow's Weeds, A Widow's Words

Lead me from the unreal to the real. Lead me from darkness to light.

The Upanishads

John was to be stationed in Okinawa, Japan, for about four months. I just knew he was pounding a typewriter. I was marking off each day on the calendar in anticipation of the week after Thanksgiving 1968, when John would return home. I was so lonesome for him.

While running errands the first weekend in August, I found John the most beautifully styled summer jacket at a department-store sale. I knew he'd be so handsome in it on our trip to the Bahamas that winter. He thought his religious calling demanded he wear black, blue and gray. Boring!

We were engaged before he told me he was a Baptist minister. After we married, I started buying his clothes with fashion ideas from *GQ*. He almost lost it when I bought him French-style underwear in colors. He was happy in plain white military-issue underwear. *Yuck.* I told him those were for me to look at and enjoy. Sometime later, he told my dad that I'd bought him the colorful underwear, and my father placed an order for some, too.

I also managed to find some his-and-hers outfits. After all, he was to be out of the Marine Corps on New Year's Eve. Our civilian life was to begin with a big bang. Since he was a Baptist minister and part of the Progressive Baptist Church in Nashville, I knew we'd not have much time to ourselves. I was making plans to meet him on his way home, store his gear and escape into our private space for a week or so in the Bahamas.

The mail from him was sporadic. He told me about how beautiful the world was. He also sent me a thank-you letter for being his wife. How strange. He mentioned that he had not had a chance to find me the promised pearls and silk in the colors I liked.

The next week, a letter came with an address change. He was in Vietnam.

I'd been feeling uneasy recently. Was it the New Jersey humidity? Was it being lonesome? On Tuesday, I went to work and felt worse. I'd never felt this way before. I went out to lunch alone. Until the day I die, I'll never forget hearing my husband's voice calling out to me as I walked back into my company's building. It was so real that I spun around looking to see where the sound came from.

On Saturday, August 10, I had an early doctor's appointment and was happy that I got a clean bill of health. I still felt miserable. I took a long, hot bath—yes, in the middle of the day in the New Jersey humidity. That was no help. I put on fresh clothes. My spirit told me to put his two favorite records on the stereo. He had bought the classics in Italy.

We'd decorated our living room in Mediterranean colors and furniture. I stretched out on the sofa and felt his presence in the music. The inner door was open to the street, and the screen door was locked. Before the second record dropped, I heard footsteps coming up the walk. The doorbell rang.

There were three U.S. Marines in summer khaki dress. I stared. "Oh, no!" automatically spilled from my mouth.

"May we come in?" asked the major. I opened the door and watched them remove their covers. All I remember was the major saying, "We are sorry. . . ." I know that I stopped the music at some point. John had died on Tuesday local time, and I heard his voice New Jersey time at about the time he took his last breath.

The words rendered by the marines were tender and sincere. I could hear people gathering outside our home. I remember yelling on the phone for my father to come to our house and not telling him why. When Dad did arrive, his arthritis did not keep him from bolting up the steps.

Plans, arrangements, phone calls. The Marine Corps was going to do this. I had to do that. The marines left, and I was alone with my painful thoughts and aching heart, along with my dad, and, now, a crowd of neighbors in my home. I'd seen my dad cry only once before, and that was at my mother's funeral. He thought my husband was the greatest thing since sliced bread.

There was no rest. We waited days for his body to arrive from the military embalming center in Dover, Delaware. The marines practically took up residence in my living room. They were protecting me from those who might have been against the Vietnam War. They had warned me about opening mail from those I did not know. I was fortunate that all the unknown senders were so kind.

Finally, my dad and I flew to Nashville. I had my first look at John in the funeral home, and it was a horror. He was sealed in glass, and I could not touch him. Only his eyebrows and long eyelashes were recognizable. I was told that the heat, time and injuries made him look that way.

If only I could have touched his gloved hand . . . "No." "How about a button?" "No." His escort was kind, but had his orders. The funeral home had its orders from the Marine Corps.

His mentor, Dr. Powell, was eloquent. The funeral was over. I followed the steel-gray, flag-covered casket to the church entry. The marine pallbearers took the earthly remains to the hearse for packaging to fly to Arlington National Cemetery the next morning.

Upon arriving in Arlington, Dad and I were taken to the chapel where we took our seats with relatives. The chaplain did the Final Rites, the gun salute, the folding of the flag and that much-said line of condolence: "On behalf of the president of the United States . . ." I received the flag, so hot from being in the sun. I asked the chaplain if I could kiss John good-bye. He said, "Yes." He escorted me to the coffin. I kissed it and whispered a message to my darling.

I sobbed all the way to my grand-aunt's home where there were more relatives awaiting us. After a couple of hours, some relatives were ready to drive my dad and me back to New Jersey. One of them reached for my still-hot flag to put it in the trunk of the car. I lost it. Never would John's flag be in the trunk of any car. Just hours earlier, I'd seen his crated casket roll out of the belly of an airplane. I clutched the flag tightly during the entire trip.

I had to move from our home. I couldn't live there without him. I rented a small townhouse. The marines were still checking on me. We had a medal presentation in the townhouse. They returned some of his belongings; the most important was his wedding ring, still caked in mud and his blood. I've never cleaned it. I removed my matching ring and put them together . . . forever.

For those who have lost and those who may lose family members, God bless you.

Patricia Barbee

I'll Be There with You

No matter where you go
or what you do,
Always remember
I'm right there with you.

I'll be there in the morning
whenever you rise,
and there in the evening
as the moon fills the skies.

I'll be there in your thoughts
and in your dreams.
Keep that in mind
no matter how bad it seems.

And if you should need me
I'll be easy to find,
Just search all the memories
you have in your mind.

I'll be with you always
as I was from the start,
I'll be there in the love
we've shared in your heart!

Tracy Atkins

9

BEYOND THE CALL OF DUTY

My life is my message.

Mahatma Gandhi

Happiness Was Born a Twin

Upon awakening every morning, I ask my higher power to use me for something greater than myself.

Oprah Winfrey

When my husband came home on a stormy February day and told me we were being transferred to Korea for a two-year tour of duty, the weather and my mood were a close match. I couldn't imagine taking our five children so far away. Our oldest son was planning on entering a nearby college that fall, the baby was barely a year old, and the other children were doing well in school. Our family life was humming along nicely, and the thought of a transfer to Korea was frightening. I entertained the idea of remaining in the States while my husband served a "bachelor tour" for one year. But my husband was determined that we should go as a family. We tossed the ball of indecision back and forth for over a week, but, in my heart, I knew we belonged together. Reluctantly, I packed kids, dishes and household items, and we were off to the Far East.

When we landed sixteen hours later, culture shock took over. On the way to our compound, we saw naked children playing in the dirt by the side of the road, and curious women peeking out from tiny shacks. The odor of open sewers permeated the air, and I wondered if my decision to spend two years in this part of the world was a wise one. But our quarters were comfortable, and we began to settle in.

I had barely managed to unpack the dishes when Ann, our chaplain's wife, called to see if I would accompany her to the Boc gum Wonn Orphanage. I really didn't want to go, but, as none of the other women from the chapel volunteered, I agreed. Ann picked me up that afternoon. With our arms full of fish that she bought at the market, we bumped along as Joe, the medic, maneuvered the Jeep along the rutted roads.

"Boc gum Wonn is the poorest of the orphanages in Taegu," Ann told me. "The children are those that no other orphanage will take."

As the Jeep swerved in the curve of the road, Ann shook her head. "It's sad to see, but the kids watch for us every week." She pointed to a hill on our left. I glanced up and saw a row of tiny figures lined up like tin soldiers. They didn't wave. They just waited.

As Joe and Ann unloaded the groceries and started up the hill, I hesitated. I knew I didn't want to see what was inside that ramshackle building, but eventually I followed along. Inside, Joe held a tiny boy in his arms.

"I call him Little Joe," he said, "because he waits for me every week. He can't walk because he is too weak."

The kids were dressed in thin shirts, in spite of the chilly October weather. The building was cold and damp, with dirt floors and cardboard in the windows to keep out the wind. The tiny building housed forty kids. Ann was handing out graham crackers to grasping hands, and

I asked her why some of those children weren't in the hospital.

"Unless they're on the verge of death, they won't accept them," she told me. A little girl beside Ann asked for another cracker. Ann smiled, "Oh, this little girl I call Lulu because of Lulu in the funnies . . . you know, big round face and round, sad eyes"

And then I saw the saddest one of all. He was skin and bones, and reminded me of the figures my kids drew in kindergarten, the ones with lines for body, arms and legs—a stick figure. I nudged Ann.

"Why isn't he in the hospital?" I asked in disbelief.

"Oh, he won't live through the week," she answered. I felt tears welling up and knew that I'd never make this trip again. The anguish was too much.

Through the next week, I kept myself busy organizing our house and getting to know our neighbors. But, at night, when we sat down for dinner, in my mind's eye, I saw Lulu, Little Joe and the Stick Boy reaching out to me. And, the next week, I was beside Ann as she headed to the orphanage. This time, I was looking forward to handing out the crackers, and sliced oranges, too. I began writing to my church back home, asking for anything they could send that would help our orphans. A remarkable chain of events ensued. Our church contacted other churches, and, soon, our service porch was up to the ceiling with boxes from the States, boxes filled with warm clothing, canned goods, medical supplies, blankets and toys . . . all for our Boc gum Wonn Orphanage.

There were so many boxes that soon the White Lily Orphanage, run by the Catholic Church, also enjoyed the bounty that flowed into Taegu. Within a couple of months, my husband contacted CHOW (Christian Hope for Orphans of the World), and they sent boatloads of canned soups and medical supplies into Inchon. These were picked up by the Korean Air Force and flown into Taegu; all these goods were targeted not only for Boc gum Wonn, but also for other orphanages, hospitals and old-age homes. The following year, we were privileged to witness the opening of the new Boc gum Wonn orphanage, built by the city of Taegu for its poorest forgotten children.

Too soon, our two years were up, and, as we took off from Taegu, I realized that only by stepping out of my comfortable lifestyle had I been privileged to become a part of these other lives. As we headed home, I knew what Lord George Gordon Byron said was true: "All who joy would win, must share it. . . . Happiness was born a twin."

Mary E. Dess

Combat Boots to Keds

*When you least expect it, someone may actu-
ally listen to what you have to say.*

Maggie Kuhn

This is the story of my almost guilt-free transformation
to professional mom.

In 1997, I moved from Andrews Air Force Base to the
home my husband and I owned near Pope Air Force Base.
My husband had been living there for months, and we
were relieved that the long weekend commutes to see
each other were finally over.

Shortly after getting settled, I was chatting on the porch
with a neighbor. "Oh, you're definitely a candidate for
postpartum depression," she said. "I had it for a whole year
after my first kid was born. If you end up crying all day, go
see a doctor." Ignoring hormonal factors, her prediction
was based solely on the fact that I was "making too many
changes." Moving, giving up my military career, having a
baby: by her calculations, it all added up to doom.

But I was excited about my new life. Finally living with
my husband and pregnant with our first child—I had long

looked forward to this. I was proud to have served my country, but, truth be told, I'd lost my enthusiasm for my job. So, while I respected my active-duty-mom friends, I harbored few doubts about my decision to resign. Besides, I assured myself, I wasn't giving up on having a profession; this was simply a career change. I'd teach at a local college—part-time at first—and increase my hours as the baby became more independent. It was a perfect arrangement.

I was right, in part. I didn't suffer a bit of depression after the baby was born. I relished every minute with him. In fact, my biggest struggle was leaving him even for a few hours with a trusted neighbor. While I enjoyed teaching, I loved being home even more. Gradually, I cut back my hours until I'd given up teaching entirely.

Still, I struggled with guilt. Despite my husband's support and assurances that his paycheck alone was sufficient, I wanted to contribute. So, on to Plan B: join the ranks of military wives with successful home businesses. I sold children's books; I sold educational toys; I sold scrapbooking supplies. With each venture, my product discount was more than I could resist. I was my own best customer. Eventually, I had to accept that my business losses were excessive and that, as a salesperson, I stunk.

By the time our daughter was born in 2000, I was half-heartedly pondering a Plan C. Finally, I relented. My career would be on hold until the children were older. The most compelling vindication for this new plan came to me as I sat at our kitchen table completing a life-insurance application. What would it cost to replace me? Never before had I tried to equate my role at home with a monetary value. Enumerating my many and varied duties was indeed a sobering exercise. In fact, I concluded that I couldn't be replaced by a single hired hand. On a piece of scratch paper, I thoughtfully assembled and priced out my team of professional replacements: a caregiver who could work lots and lots of overtime, a cook, a tutor, a housekeeper, a driver, a secretary, a gardener, a book-keeper . . . Soon, I felt like Wonder Mom, a wonderfully underpaid Wonder Mom. And I prayed that my family would never need that insurance.

Then, picking up my son at preschool one day, I noticed he was more animated than usual. "Mom!" he exclaimed breathlessly. "Kate's mother was in the army!"

In fact, I knew that Kate's mom had been in the service. So had Nicolas's mom, a former helicopter pilot; and Eugenie's mom, a former army surgeon; and Olivia's mom, a former army nurse. At preschool, I've also met civilian moms who've given up or scaled back their careers—an accountant, a teacher, a speech pathologist. There are also working moms, incredibly talented women who somehow manage that seemingly impossible balance between family and career. And, of course, there are those fortunate ones who've always known that being a mom was all they really wanted.

Kate's mom had been invited to school to talk about being a jumpmaster. She'd shown the kids a video of herself and others parachuting from a plane. Then, she arranged the chairs in the classroom to represent a miniature version of the inside of a C-130, and the kids pretended to jump as she called the commands. My son was starstruck!

Then it dawned on me—my own kids didn't even know that I had a life before they did. I'd been an air force personnel officer and an army intelligence analyst. Yikes! Suddenly, nine years of dedicated service in the world's greatest military seemed like pretty ho-hum stuff. No doubt, my preschooler would rate my story as compara-tively lacking in hooah. But he should know the truth: His mother had never felt compelled to jump out of a plane—for fun or any other reason.

That afternoon, with some trepidation, I dusted off my old scrapbook. The time had come to show my children that their mother (yes, I'm going to say it) wore combat boots. But that scrapbook! To me, it represented a life so distant, it seemed that somebody else had lived it.

As I opened it, I thought of the years I'd spent cultivating a new role for myself: professional mom. Sure, it isn't for everyone, but for me, the job satisfaction is unbeatable and the benefits too numerous to quantify—and, often, too deeply personal to express. So I don't try. Let's just say that I'm grateful to finally have found a job that I love.

Seeing my children's faces as they gazed over photos of a younger me, wearing a uniform ("Hey, like Dad's!") was a revelation. That was me: a "chair-born stranger." But my kids were impressed . . . and proud. My son said I was cool.

And, at that moment, it was clear to me that my life hadn't become just a series of interrupted careers. Now, I see a defined route that led me to who I am today. Sure, I've made a lot of changes in my life, but with these I've gained fascinating experiences and learned invaluable lessons. I have so much to teach my children—about the world, about people, about what's important in life.

"Did you like being a soldier?" my son wanted to know. It was a test question.

"Yes, but I like being home with you now."

He looked up at me with a reassuring smile, revealing an understanding that belied his young age.

"I like being home with you, too," he said. My son has his father's knack for finding a few simple words that can melt my heart.

The children didn't dwell on the photos long. As their interest waned, they began turning the pages more quickly. Caring for little ones doesn't allow much time for personal indulgences, like peaceful recollections of one's youth. I sat back and watched the remnants of my former life fly by until the book was closed, and my kids proclaimed it lunchtime.

Then I returned my scrapbook to the top of the bookcase where tiny fingers would find it out of reach. Out of sight. Out of mind. Right where it belongs.

Debbie Koharik

Welcome Home!

The day had finally arrived and my husband, Andy, was due home from a tour-of-duty in Korea. A veteran of World War II, Andy was a captain with the Air Force and had been fighting in Korea for nearly a year and a half. The kids and I had really missed him.

Wanting to look our Sunday best upon Andy's arrival, but not having the money to purchase new clothes from the department store for myself and our two young children, I scraped together enough material to make us clothes. I sewed a cute outfit for our daughter, Scharre, and a jacket and tie for our son, Bryan, and had just enough left to make myself a knee-length, white lace dress, just like a young bride's gown. We looked spiffy!

At the airport, the three of us gathered with the other families waiting for husbands, fathers, brothers and friends. Excitement filled the large air-hanger as the plane landed! Our boys were finally home!

About two hundred troops deplaned and instantly went into formation at the commander's orders of "attention!" The men looked weary, tired, bedraggled, but from what I could read on their faces, they were happy and relieved to be home. After a few moments in formation, the commander ordered them into an "at ease" stance.

Before the commander could issue another order, I worked my way through the crowd, with Scharre and Bryan in tow, and approached him.

"Excuse me, sir. I would like to address the men, please," I told the commander. Before he could utter a word, I faced the troops.

"Welcome home! Welcome home! Welcome home!" I said in a loud voice, turning in a different direction with each "welcome" so all the men could hear me. "Don't you look wonderful! We are so happy you have returned safe-and-sound! Thank you for your service to your country! Again, welcome home!"

I looked at the commander—his mouth agape in disbelief at my moxie—and thanked him. Taking the children's hands, I rejoined the other families.

Still stunned, the commander squared himself and called his troops back to attention. After a very long second, he yelled "dismissed!" Not one of those two hundred men moved a single muscle—the entire hanger was silent and still, waiting to see which soldier would step forward to claim the lady in the white lace dress.

With his head held high, Andy made his way toward us through the frozen formation. Scharre and Bryan, recognizing their father, ran to meet him. Andy bent down and gave each of the children a big bear hug and kiss, then he proudly walked over to me. Again, the men and their families stood in complete silence.

Andy gave me a big kiss on the lips and everyone cheered! It was just like our wedding day with the guests waiting for that special closing smooch. At that instant, the troops fell out of formation, running to their families to do the same, with laughter and shouts of jubilation filling the air.

A handsome pilot had returned to his young bride. He was home, for good.

DeEtta Woffinden Anderson,
as told to Dahlynn McKowen

A Colorful Experience

I'm not afraid of storms, for I'm learning how to sail my own ship.

Louisa May Alcott

I cannot figure out why they call us "military depen-dents," since we are actually "military independents," although not necessarily by choice. In the military hand-book, chapter 6, section 2, paragraph 3A, it states that the husband should plan the transfers and/or deployments so the spouse has to make all the arrangements without him. Just kidding! *There is no such handbook!* I'm just say-ing that most of us have experienced that kind of chal-lenge at least once in a military career, and we just make it happen, and, most likely, two or three years later, we make it happen again.

Color me independent.

The first year we were married, my husband asked me what I wanted for Christmas. I replied nonchalantly (like this was every woman's dream), "a variable-speed reversible drill." He got the biggest kick from my response, but thought that was the greatest thing (especially since a shipmate's wife wanted a diamond ring and a fur coat). Well, he got me the drill for Christmas—a Craftsman from Sears, no less—and I've made good use of it at *every* duty station. (Sometimes, I even let him use it.)

Color me practical.

Window furnishings, especially with a variety of window sizes at each duty station, can get quite expensive. Well, I came up with the idea of using plastic shower curtains on the inside curtain rod and dressing it up with inexpensive white or beige sheers on the outer rod. In Adak, Alaska, where sun is scarce, I hung bright-yellow shower curtains in the dining room. When the daylight would shine through the yellow, it looked like the sun was shining outside. It was a great pick-me-up since dreary days can really bring you down. At the next duty station, "practical me" used my drill to hang or redo the curtain rods, "independent me" bought new shower curtains (different colors to coordinate with the new environment), and I used the same sheers. But wait—don't throw the old shower curtains away! They make great drop cloths for household cleaning, carpentry, kids' craft projects, and, of course, painting all those welcome-home signs for the guys returning from months of deployment.

Color me resourceful.

Families always try to do special things for their guy when he is deployed. At the family monthly support-group meetings, we'd hang up white bed sheets, one for each deployment site (don't know who came up with this clever idea), and the wives and children would write messages or draw pictures for their spouse/daddy. It was especially nice to make different ones for the different holidays. The sheets were hung in the galleys at each deployment site, so, during chow time, all the guys could look for their personal message from their loved ones— an extra-special touch of home.

Color us creative.

The guys were deployed to Desert Shield/Storm through Thanksgiving, Christmas, New Year's and Easter, so they received several message sheets. When my man came home and was unpacking, he handed me what seemed to be some bunched-up rags. I pulled them apart and discovered he cut out all my messages from the sheets and brought them home! How sweet! I was so touched. Many of the other husbands did the same thing. I'd surely like to have a video of the men cutting up those sheets.

Color them full of surprises!

I'm going to include those message cutouts in a memory quilt I'm planning to make someday when I'm retired. It will be sewn from high-school sports letters, presidential fitness patches, and logo cutouts from T-shirts and sweat-shirts from every duty station, command, and running race that my husband participated in. (Also, pieces of lin-gerie, but don't tell my husband—I'm full of surprises, too!)

Color me imaginative!

I love living on base. I can't describe the sensation I feel when I see the troops running by and hearing them shouting out cadence at o'dark-thirty; the pride and goose bumps I experience seeing the American flag being raised every morning and lowered every evening. The "Star Spangled Banner" and "God Bless the USA" choke me up and bring tears to my eyes no matter how many times I hear them played. Since 9/11, every day, I've worn some combination of a red, white and blue ribbon with a variety of patriotic pins and a yellow ribbon. It's in mem-ory of those who died that day, in honor of the rescue workers, in support of our troops, in tribute to those who made the ultimate sacrifice ensuring our freedom and in pride of our wonderful country.

Color me proud to be a military spouse and an American!

Nancy Hall

Patriotic Women Bake Cookies

I think somehow we learn who we really are and then live with that decision.

Eleanor Roosevelt

"What do you want me to do? Stay home and bake cookies?" That could have been me twenty years ago. I was a thoroughly modern woman. Newly married to an air force pilot, I was not going to be shackled by outdated images of the proper officer's wife. I was not going to be one of those squadron wives who scurried around making wonderful home-baked goodies for the "cookie bus" during combat exercises. I scoffed at the squadron commander's wife who exhorted us to keep cookie dough in the freezer so we would be ready to go whenever the exercises kicked off. How silly! Our husbands are training to go to war. They don't care about chocolate chips and snickerdoodles!

Now look at me: Twenty years later, I am the commander's wife and I have my apron on. I am rolling out sugar cookies for the airmen who will be in the dorms for the holidays. Other wives are churning out chocolate-chip cookies to send with deploying troops. I've got cookie dough in my freezer! Why do military wives bake cookies? After twenty years, I understand.

When I married my husband, I accepted his choice to be an air force pilot, but that was his job, not mine. Over the years, I have learned that his choice is more than a job. It is a mission. I have watched as military careers ended when a spouse could not accept the demands of the mission. I have watched as marriages ended when a soldier could not give up the mission. Therefore, I have embraced the mission in my own way.

I cannot fly or fix the planes. I don't carry a weapon. But I can volunteer my hands and heart to those who do. And I can bake cookies. They are baked with flour, sugar, butter and a lot of prayers. I can only hope that each soldier finds some small comfort in my culinary creation. I pray he feels the respect and support my heart added to the recipe. His sacrifice for America has inspired in me a reverence for America. His willingness to defend this nation has taught me that this is a nation worth defending.

Yes, I am still a modern woman. But, now, I am a patriotic woman. And I bake cookies.

Denise J. Hunnell

"Normally, a *yellow* ribbon would be tied until he returns, but with my husband's sense of humor . . ."

Something to Be Proud Of

One is not born but rather becomes a woman.

Simone de Beauvoir

When Susan got engaged to Gary, her mum confessed many reservations about her daughter marrying a soldier. Susan's mother and I are best friends.

Within a year, Gary was posted to Ireland, and Susan couldn't go with him. A year later, she gave birth to little Innes. She spent a lot of time at her mum's house rather than live alone.

When Gary came home, it was only to tell Susan that he was being posted to Germany, and she and little Innes would be able to go with him. This move terrified Susan so much that she began to lose weight. I wondered if she would refuse to go, but the day came, and off they went.

Susan had been there for a year, when, suddenly, she arrived home with Innes, unannounced. Susan said Gary was away all the time; she was left with strangers and felt like an outsider. Gary arrived home and told his side of the story. It was obvious these two were very young, and, instead of talking over their problems, they blamed each other. Finally, they sorted it out, were back in love again, and, off they went, back to Germany.

Susan's mum went out to visit her and learned all was not well again. Susan mixed very little, just enough to show her face, and now Gary had been told that he was being posted to the Middle East. Since she couldn't join him, she immediately announced that she was coming home to wait for him in Scotland.

By this time, Susan was pregnant again, and, after Gary had been in the Middle East for two months, Kerry was born. There were regular letters between the couple, but I think both Susan's mum and I suspected that when Gary returned, things were not going to be very good between them.

It was a lovely sunny June morning when Susan's mum's telephone rang. It was military headquarters, and they had been trying to get in touch with Susan. Gary had been wounded and was in the hospital. They would fly him back to Germany within the next few days. They asked if he couldn't be flown back to the United Kingdom, but were told that his injury was quite serious and the specialist was based in Hamburg.

"What is his injury?" Susan asked in a flat voice.

"He has been blinded," came the short reply.

Susan bit her lip and asked, "Is it a temporary thing?"

There was a pause. "Mrs. Phillips, that is unlikely, but the specialist will decide."

Susan and her mum and dad flew to Germany that same day. Susan just couldn't imagine how Gary would cope. He was outgoing, and the army was his life. Two days later, the doctors informed them there was nothing they could do to restore his sight in either eye.

Susan cried, but, once the tears were finished, her resolve set in. Her mum said it was as if Susan suddenly grew up in that endless hospital corridor. "I want to see him and find out how soon we can get him out of hospital," she said.

She was the one who said she wanted to tell him the bad news. She held him when he cried, and she told him that they would make a new life together. She was advised that, once Gary could get out, he would still need treatment for his other wounds, and they would prefer him to stay on base in Germany until they officially released him from the army.

This was no problem for Susan; she had her mum bring both the children over so that Gary could have something to absorb his interest a little. Susan took complete control. She nursed Gary mentally and physically. She looked after the two young children, and she set out their accommodations so that Gary could find his way about. This meant it had to be free of toys and clutter. She liaised with the doctors and with the army as to what was the next best step for Gary.

She pleaded with the army to find something that a blind man could do for them, but, finally, they returned to the United Kingdom. Instead of coming home to Scotland, Susan had other ideas. She felt that Gary would give up if he sat at home doing nothing all day.

She talked someone in the army into giving them accommodations near a camp in the South of England, and, with her encouragement, Gary found a job on a helpline for the army.

Our admiration for Susan is enormous. Gary is back in control again, but she is always there in the background, ready to give support when needed. Whenever anyone says anything to her about how her life has turned out, she just shrugs and says, "All part of being an army wife. Gary is alive, and we have two wonderful kids. I never forget that Gary got hurt fighting for his country and that was why he joined the army in the first place. It's something I am very proud of."

Joyce Stark

The Wedding

We often look so long and so regretfully at the closed door that we do not notice the one which has opened for us.

Helen Keller

I was going to have the perfect wedding. With May 6, 2000, on its way, my mother and I were actively planning for the "event of the century," as we liked to call it. We would talk every day, and discussing the wedding plans made the two of us especially giddy, like nothing we had ever shared.

At the time, I was finishing up my commitment to the navy at Great Lakes Naval Training Center, and had been in a long-distance relationship with my fiancé, Paul, for the past three years. We met in Bath, Maine, where we were both part of the commissioning crews of two different guided missile destroyers.

The trick was that his ship was being stationed in Pearl Harbor, Hawaii, and mine was going to Mayport, Florida. We had been engaged for two years, so time was not our enemy ... but it was for my mother. She had been battling breast cancer for more than five years.

One day, my mother sat me down to talk about the possibility of her not being at my wedding. I had been telling her all along that she was the reason I was making such a spectacle of the day. I would have been happy with a small ceremony, but Mom would not hear of it. She wanted me to have everything I had ever dreamed of.

I only had two dreams growing up. One was to attend the Naval Academy and to throw my hat in the air with the other 895 midshipmen of the class of 1995. The other was to be married under the classic dome of the United States Naval Academy Chapel with ten men waiting outside in their starched whites, swords drawn, waiting to welcome me into married life, navy style.

So I gave her my word that I would have an "extravagant" wedding, even in her absence, because, honestly, I never thought it would come to that. I remember her hugging me after I promised and whispering in my ear, "I will have the best seat in the house on May 6." I hugged her tighter and said a little prayer right then and there. I had a great relationship with God; I didn't see any reason that he wouldn't help me with this one.

About six months later, my mother lost her fight with breast cancer. I had trouble accepting the fact that she was gone, and I kept imagining and dreaming that she would show up on my wedding day. My mom wasn't just a mom; she was my friend, my confidante and my rock. No matter what was going on in my life, with her by my side, I could accomplish anything. I just couldn't imagine life without her.

My wedding day drew nearer. The chapel, the reception and the rehearsal dinner were all set according to the plan. My fiancé and I were going to make this the perfect weekend getaway not only for us, but also for our family and friends.

I left the navy and was spending a few weeks with Paul in Hawaii before I found a job. We were at a ship function when his captain made the announcement that Paul had been dreading to share with me. The situation in the Gulf was heating up, and his ship's deployment was moved from July to April. When the captain uttered those words, my body froze and my breath shortened. My first thought was May 6, the date my mom would be at the chapel to watch her baby walk down the aisle. I know the average and sane person would assume my mom would get the word and would be there whatever date we got married. But May 6 was the date she planned to be at the chapel.

Paul's captain looked over at me, and I'll remember that moment forever. He grabbed my hand and promised he'd try to do everything in his power to have Paul there.

We went ahead with the wedding planning, and Paul and I decided that we'd go ahead with the celebration, with or without his presence. He deployed to the Gulf as newly scheduled, on April 6. Every spare minute I had I was locked onto the headlines as I prayed for peace and for no events to stand in the way of his flight to Washington.

My dad, my sister, Katie, and I all met in Annapolis to do the last-minute planning. My mother's absence was glaring. On our arrival, we went to visit the chapel, which was open and empty. We walked through the large doors and stood at the back, staring up at the breathtaking colors of the stained glass that fills the space with spirituality.

All of a sudden, "Taps" began playing. There was no one around, no one playing on the organ, no one checking out the acoustics of the dome, just "Taps" playing loudly, echoing through the chapel. We walked around and then stood once again at the back. The three of us looked at each other, comforted and moved by the music. As we left, the music stopped, but the solace it gave me that day has remained with me.

God came through on my wedding day. God knew I needed something to let me know my mother was still there for me, and he gave it to me that special day in the chapel where "Taps" provided me the most comfort of all. It was then that I understood that she was with me not only on that day, but always.

God gave me a mother who built my wedding dream with me, who touched my life and continues to touch my life in amazing ways. He gave Paul and me a courageous and understanding commanding officer who truly understood that, if at all possible, navy families come first. Paul's captain is my hero.

Paul made the wedding.

Krystee Kott

Angel in the Air

I feel we are all islands in a common sea.

Anne Morrow Lindbergh

In February 2003 my husband was given leave to fly to Georgia and help me move cross-country to our new duty station in Texas. This was during the time of the War on Terror, when the threat of war with Iraq was beginning to look like a reality. Protestors were coming together all over the world. People were expressing their views in newspapers, proclaiming that they had no pity for the troops. My brother-in-law was already serving in Afghanistan, and we were uncertain whether or not my husband would be deployed to the Middle East. Suddenly, I didn't feel like the sacrifices we were making for our country were worth it.

He had been sent to Texas with little warning and sent back to Georgia with not much more. He didn't have any civilian clothes with him, so, when he boarded the plane, he was dressed in the daily "BDUs," camouflage clothes. As he got off the plane, one of the flight attendants handed him a small piece of paper. It read:

When you stepped onto my airplane you brought tears to my eyes. My little brother is currently a U.S. Army soldier serving in Kuwait, and, just by chance, our last name is Johnson also. I appreciate your presence and wish you nothing but the best. You are a hero to me, and I thank you for all that you are.

God bless! From the bottom of my heart, know you are loved.

Your thankful flight attendant,
Shannon Johnson

I read this note over several times, each time fighting back tears a little more. I've never known how to express exactly what that letter did for me. But, after reading it, I knew that my husband was appreciated, that our struggle wasn't going unnoticed. I knew that I shared that struggle with so many other military spouses and family members, and I no longer had to carry that burden alone.

Ramiah Johnson

It Took a War

We do not see things as they are, we see them as we are.

The Talmud

I was a helicopter pilot in the U.S. Army when I married my husband, an army armor officer. I did not want to be labeled "family dependent," as they called us back then. I was a pilot, a strong woman, not just somebody's dependent. For years, I refused to call myself an "army wife."

Over the next decade, as my husband progressed through the ranks, I begrudgingly wore the required proverbial hats of "XO's wife" and the "commander's wife," hating the titles for what I thought they implied: I was the subordinate sidekick to my husband's career. I proudly maintained my identity based on my post-army career as a writer.

"Do you think you're a good army wife?" a young wife asked me one day. I was shocked at her question. Did she think I thought I was? Did she think I wasn't?

"Why do you ask?" I queried in reply.

"Because I think you are, and I want to be as good an army wife as you are." I was shocked.

"I never . . . ," I said haltingly. "I never really considered myself an army wife."

A few years later, in 2003—now at a new duty station and yet another job position—my husband left for Kuwait and Operation Iraqi Freedom. Over the next few months, I cried, laughed, prayed, worked, played and spent hours on the phone with other "army wives" from my husband's unit. We tied yellow ribbons, we shared information of our husbands' whereabouts, and we consoled one another. We handled finances, crashing computers, stalling cars, worried children, midnight crying fests and overgrown lawns. We were the strongest we had ever been—we had no other choice. For the first time in my marriage, I knew what it truly meant to be an "army wife." And I was proud to be one.

It took a war to make me realize how important the "army wife" is to the military—how important everything is that we, as military spouses, do to support our husbands, the army and our country. I saw that I could have other interests, other careers, and still be a great "army wife." Everywhere I went, I wanted others to know my husband was off to war, fighting for our freedom as well as those of an oppressed country. Waiting to pick up friends at the airport, in line at the store, or wherever I was, civilians' chatter always turned to the war in Iraq.

"I'm an army wife," I'd say to them. "Let me tell you what it's like. . . ."

Jan Hornung

10

LIVING YOUR DREAM

What lies behind us and what lies before us are tiny matters compared to what lies within us.

Ralph Waldo Emerson

Change of Perspective

You cannot make yourself feel something you do not feel, but you can make yourself do right in spite of your feelings.

Pearl S. Buck

I'd been preparing myself for this moment for weeks, and I still wasn't ready for the feelings of anxiety and fear that overcame me on the day he left.

In the winter of 1997, my family was stationed at Holloman Air Force Base in New Mexico. My husband, a helicopter pilot, was part of the 48th Search and Rescue squadron, and he was getting ready for his first deployment to the Middle East. All through the day, a dark cloud hung over me. I was starting to question his commitment to his country, and I was wondering if it was really worth the pain of this separation.

That evening, as my daughter Sabrina was setting the dinner table, she took four plates out of the cabinet: one for her, one for her brother Nick, one for me and one for her father. As she realized her error, and that her father would not be home for dinner that evening, we both gave in to tears.

In an effort to lighten the mood, I took my children to an evening performance of an air force group called Tops in Blue. Their performance promised an evening of patriotic songs and dance routines, and hundreds of us packed into the local community center in our red, white and blue sweaters.

All around me, I saw other military spouses and their children, as well as many members of our civilian community, smiling in anticipation of the evening's show. Everyone appeared to be in good spirits, and I wondered what was wrong with me and why I was questioning my allegiance to the USA. I just wasn't feeling patriotic.

It was at this low moment that the colors of the flag were presented, and we rose to sing the national anthem. As I stood there with my hand listlessly over my heart, I noticed an elderly gentleman in a wheelchair about fifteen feet from me.

The first strains of the anthem began, and the gentleman waved toward two of the ushers flanking the stadium sides. The uniformed airmen hurried to his side, and I wondered if he was feeling unwell. They leaned down so the gentleman could whisper his request into their ears, and then gently lifted him out of his wheelchair, supporting his body so he could stand and salute the flag. Our flag.

I looked at my children, and I saw the awe and reverence with which they watched this wonderful man. In that moment, I felt a flash of understanding and a deep sense of shame that I had doubted my husband's choice to serve in the air force and my commitment as a military spouse. Tears began to stream down my face.

During future deployments, this gentleman became a reminder to me of what it is all about. His example gave me the dose of courage that I needed.

Sonja R. Ragaller

Identity: A Time of Transition

Life is change. Growth is optional. Choose wisely.

Karen Kaiser Clark

Sweat dripped from my forehead as I pulled the last items from the bottom of the dishpack in our new quarters. The coffee mugs strewn on the kitchen counter represented our travel, activities, interests and all nine assignments for the past twenty-three years. I smiled when I unwrapped the plastic Winnie the Pooh dish our three boys had used as toddlers.

No more plastic dishes now that all three boys attended college in northern California. My husband, Denny, and I had moved to our final assignment at Edwards Air Force Base in the southern part of that very long state. We worked at our own pace, with no need to cook huge meals or investigate the schools. We missed the laughter, the extra hands and the muscles, yet we intended to enjoy the novelty of an empty nest.

Coming from a house off base, the two of us could live in this smaller space. No problem—until we tried to fit in furniture for five. We still had their three dressers, three beds, a weight bench, out-of-season clothes, skis and tons of memorabilia. The pianist was at college playing water polo, living in a dorm room. Where could we put that piano? Frustrated, we shoved it against an inside wall in the dining room.

Slowly, I realized that this tiny house, overflowing with boxes and stuff, was vast, vacant and too quiet. Just the two of us.

We moved on to other tasks. "Twink, do you still want your toys kept in the hall closet?" Denny's voice came from inside a large box.

My toys! Years ago, our sons collected the surviving preschool toys—wooden blocks, a few Fisher-Price faithfuls, books and small trucks—and dubbed them "Mom's toys." For the last fourteen years, these relics lived in hall closets, available when little ones happened into our home. "Yes, please. In the hall closet, down on the floor, just like always. Soon, neighbors will drop by, and their kids can play with my toys."

But no young mothers came. For a year, the remnant of my identity lay in the hall closet with those toys. I met young mothers at church and base functions. They chatted about schools and teachers, disposable diapers and teething, about the soccer game and Boy Scouts. I listened; I understood. After all, I'd been there. But they didn't know I knew. My gray hair seemed to say I didn't care about children.

As the young moms talked, my heart remembered. Our boys had so many teachers at twelve different schools. Boy Scouts? I served as a den mother in two countries and raised two Eagle Scouts. Trips to the emergency room? Plenty. Sports? T-ball, baseball, basketball, football, swimming, tennis, water polo, track, cross-country, soccer. Late dinners and carpooling. Piano lessons and driving lessons. I'd witnessed the heartache of their friends moving away, or, worse yet, uprooting our boys away from friends. First dates, late dates and sweetheart separations. *I know! Ask me!* my heart cried.

At previous assignments, where people knew our boys, mothers asked me how to handle thorny situations. But these new friends didn't know about our three sons; we were simply the old couple who moved in down the street.

The year dragged. One irksome problem harassed me: *Who am I?* I'd lost my identity and couldn't pull it out of the past. While *I* hadn't changed, my circumstances had. People didn't understand or care who I had been.

We escaped our lonely situation by traveling up and down the state to watch our youngest son play water polo. After the games, we spent time with him, and, often, his devoted girlfriend joined us. One afternoon, I looked at this tall young man, full of excitement for the future, and realized his life was moving ahead much faster than ours. Yes, we would always be his parents, people whom he could count on for love and help. But he no longer needed me to watch over him.

Then, I understood. My role as mother had undergone a complete makeover. My past will always be a part of me and help me understand others. But I must concentrate on who I am, the woman people know today. I had to get to know this new me.

For twenty-some years, caring for family had taken precedence over other roles. But I had found time to work at the thrift shop and family services. I participated in Protestant Women of the Chapel and taught Sunday school. I could assimilate those experiences with new interests and long-forgotten hopes and dreams. Just as motherhood evolved as the boys grew, the new me would develop into a more complete woman.

It took time, perhaps six months, to discover living in the present far surpasses living in the past. Occasionally, when I pulled a jacket out of the hall closet, I'd see my old toys. I'd straighten my shoulders and smile. My identity no longer resided in those tattered toys.

Identity, I learned, is not who I was, but who I am.

Twink DeWitt

If I Return

The silence that accepts merit as the most natural thing in the world is the highest applause.

Ralph Waldo Emerson

If I return from battle, I do not know if I will stand alone or be helped by a comrade.

I do not know if my limbs will be there or if my eyes will see.

But I will know deep within my soul that I have served my country and that I have set man free.

I would like to see the yellow ribbons, worn in your hair, on your lapels or on the "old oak tree."

I would like to know that they are worn with pride and that you truly prayed for me.

To know that you supported me in everything that I did when I obeyed the high command.

I was doing what man has done to free the world of tyranny.

When I left I was in my youth, too young to vote or buy a beer.

When I returned, aged, worn and tired, seeing too much, being alone and truly knowing fear.

Yes, I was in harm's way, I did not have the opportunity to ask why.

Was it because what I did would make man free or was it because freedom would pass me by?

Free to know that in my heart I have pride in my fellow man and myself.

Proud to know that I have served my country and my country is still a free land.

If you see me on the street, will you call me a baby killer?

Will you spit on my uniform when you see the battle ribbons on my chest?

If you cannot take my hand and say "well done," pass me when we meet.

For I have served you and my country, and I have served my very best.

Sharon C. Stephens Trippe

Lollipops

My religion is loving-kindness.

The Dalai Lama

It was 1971, and I was a senior in college. About two months after I started dating George, the man I was going to marry, he came over to my parents' home and asked if I minded if he joined the National Guard. The Vietnam War had been going on for several years. I didn't approve of the war but I only took part in one antiwar protest, a silent walk to a local park to hear a few speakers, and I never really gave much thought of him being activated if he did join.

George left for boot camp and schooling in March 1972 and returned in July. I was busy with student teaching and trying to finish my degree. We continued on with our lives, and George was never called in to serve in the war. He remained in the guards, and I supported him because the money was good and I could tell that he really enjoyed it.

In 1991, when the Gulf War broke out, I was really nervous, but luckily it ended in pretty short order. He said that, had it gone on a few more days, he was certain that he would have been activated. Before we knew it, he had been in for thirty-two years and was the first sergeant for his artillery unit, a job he really enjoyed.

Several legislators proposed that the retirement age for the military be dropped to fifty-five. We loved the idea, and it would only be another three years before George turned fifty-five. I figured that I could stand the wait— after all, I had managed to survive this long.

In November 2003, rumors flew that his unit was to be deployed. It was true, but he was not included. I breathed a sigh of relief. I was happy because he wasn't going and because he had just retired from his full-time job. We would finally be able to spend more time together. Four days later, he came home from a meeting and told me that they had added another E8 position. I knew what that meant: My husband was being deployed. *I'm too old for this*, I thought. *And so is he.*

I had a broken finger, a cast on my hand, and my fifty-two-year-old husband was leaving me by myself. The good-byes were extremely difficult.

I went to work after he left, but I wasn't sure what to share with my high-school students. I was reluctant at first to tell them what was happening. I wanted my professional life at the school to remain separate from my personal life. That didn't last long. I felt a need to talk about what was happening, and, to my delight, the students were extremely supportive and fully understanding.

A few students had relatives or friends who were now over in the Middle East, or who had been there, and there were some who had family members who would be leaving soon. I found out that sharing was very therapeutic. They talked about their feelings about the war, and I shared stories about George, who I now called the "old man in the desert." Whenever I found a student who had a relative being deployed, I gave them a "service flag" and a pin to wear. It made me feel good, and, hopefully, helped them to know that I understood what they were going through.

My colleagues were also very supportive. I had a habit of sending Tootsie Roll Pops to my husband, and his unit gave them out to Iraqi children. The librarian thought this would be a great project for the student assistants. I asked my classes to donate pops and to drop their loose change in my Tootsie Roll bank. The librarians decorated a box in the library, and I would check to see the progress each day. It was so overwhelming. Before we knew it, we had more than four thousand Tootsie Roll Pops, as well as other types of lollipops and Tootsie Roll Midgies. I mailed out eight large boxes full of candy, and the following Monday, we received another donation of a thousand more!

The students were wonderful—they rose to the occasion. They made the time that George has been away a heck of a lot more bearable. Next school year, we are planning on collecting school supplies and soccer balls, and my students have promised to stop by and ask about my "old man in the desert." I love working with high-school students—they amaze me, they keep me young and help me forget that I am "too old for this."

Diane Proulx

Military Family

You don't live in a world all alone. Your brothers (sisters) are here, too.

Albert Schweitzer

The military is now your family.

Ten years ago, a military spouse spoke those words to me on the day I married my soldier husband. I really did not understand this comment or how true it would become in the future.

My husband kissed me good-bye on our fourth anniversary and left for a ten-month deployment to Operation Joint Guard in Bosnia. That day was one of the hardest of my life. We had spent four years trying to get pregnant, and now he was gone for almost a year.

Three weeks later, I made a miraculous discovery: We were going to have a baby. My husband called from Bosnia at three in the morning, and telling him the good news was both painful and jubilant. We had done it—and now he wouldn't be here to touch my stomach, to watch the baby grow inside me. The baby was due two months before he was to return to Fort Polk. I was going to have to do it alone. Or so I thought.

It was then that I learned what people meant when they said "military family." My friend Wanda offered to stand in as "Dad," going with me to all my appointments and recording the baby's heartbeat to send overseas. The support I got was incredible. People called me, brought me food and stopped by. My husband's Rear Detachment checked on me regularly.

One night, after returning home from working a bingo game for the Enlisted Spouses Club, I settled into bed only to have my water break. It was two weeks early, and I was terrified. I was not ready yet. Wanda came over, helped me to pack my bag and took me to the hospital. She stayed right by my side until nine that morning when they handed my little miracle to me.

I looked over and said, "Wanda, I'm a mommy." By the time I was in the recovery room, Rear Detachment had gotten a hold of my husband, and he was on the phone talking to me about our new baby boy. It was the most exciting and wonderful day of my life.

That night, Baby Jacob had some trouble with his lungs. An hour later, I was told that he had to go to Shreveport to a neonatal ICU for a problem with his colon. I was terrified. This amazing experience was becoming a terrifying nightmare.

Wanda came to the hospital, and I went with Jacob in the ambulance. In Shreveport, I called Wanda, and found out that my military family had kicked into high gear. Rear Detachment was working on reaching my husband. Some of the ladies had called my mom, gotten her a plane reservation and were making arrangements to bring her to the hospital. Someone else was taking care of the dog and the house. Another spouse had gone to the store and bought anything she could think of to help me get through my stay: bottled water, snacks (I was going to try to breast-feed), phone cards, paper, nursing pads, Tylenol, etc. One had even gotten a rosary and brought it to my chaplain to have it blessed for my son's bed in the ICU.

I was amazed at their efforts, and I no longer felt so alone. I could not believe how quickly everything had been taken care of. The only thing I had to worry about was my son. Jacob and I spent a week in neonatal ICU, then he was able to come home. The ladies continued to take care of everything for me while I was gone. The Enlisted Spouses Club I belonged to even helped out with the cost of the hotel room my mom was staying in near the hospital.

It took a week for them to get my husband all the way back to Louisiana, and, luckily, my son was released the day he got home, so Pat never had to see him in ICU. When my mom and I arrived home that Friday morning, my house had been cleaned, the nursery finished and the baby's bed made. There were even some meals in my freezer. To this day, I am still truly amazed at my military family and how well they took care of my family and me.

I have been a proud military wife for ten years now and would not change it for the world. Times have been good and times have been tough, but I have never felt alone or without support from my military family. They are wonderful. I never would have made it through this situation as well as I did without their support, love and prayers. I have strived since that day to be a military family to other spouses when they have needed me. This life we chose is not always an easy one, but we can always get through the tough times as long as we stay a military family.

It took some time, but I finally understood what that woman said to me on my wedding day: I married a military man, and his family is my family.

Shawni Sticca

Mail Call—
God's Provision for Intimacy

Loneliness is the poverty of self; solitude is the richness of self.

May Sarton

My husband and I started writing letters to each other early in our friendship. We had no choice. Before the advent of e-mail, it was write or not communicate. Fred and I met in Washington, D.C., two weeks before he left the Naval Academy for his sophomore summer midshipman training. He was onboard ship for most of that summer, so letter writing was integral in how we got to know each other. We'd send silly cards, cut out cartoons from the paper—whatever we could think of to make our next connection meaningful and fun.

Three years of dating and writing culminated in our wedding at the Naval Academy chapel on a glorious June morning, but nothing could have prepared me for the next ten years of continuous sea duty. Fred was away for days and weeks, with three-month and the killer six-month deployments.

While the ship transited the Pacific, there were no mail drops for almost four weeks, sometimes five—an eternity for a mom with two young daughters. Oh, the burst of joy at finding a much-awaited letter in the box after weeks of no communication! That single envelope with my sweetheart's handwriting on it was all it took to get me singing exultant hallelujahs you could hear clear down the block. I'd clutch the letter to my heart, running inside to savor and devour his words like a dieter gorging on a big chocolate bar. I'd read them over and over and over.

On the far side of the ocean, mail call was the highlight of every "underway replenishment," when the ship would gas up from a fuel tanker at sea. Soon, the mailbags came across the lines strung between the two ships, the sailors and officers anxiously awaiting their letters from home. Fred told me that he reacted much like I did, hoarding his precious envelopes, finding a comfortable spot at day's end to read and reread the news from home.

With two pregnancies, sick babies, a burglary, bursting pipes and being on mom duty 24/7, believe me, there were days when I wanted to scream, "Enough!" *How would our marriage survive,* I wondered many times, *with an ocean between us?* Through all the shipboard separations, our letters were the glue that connected us and held us together.

I remember (it still brings a smile) the letter from Guam that explained the ship was met by numerous brown boobies. Instantly indignant, I read on, only to learn that brown boobies were local birds!

Then there were those times I shared portions of Fred's letters with our young daughters. I read a funny story about Daddy's liberty in Hong Kong, and how he described eating "escargot," better known as snails, in a local restaurant. He'd liked them! Can you imagine that?

A few days later, when I was out working in the yard, I caught three-and-a-half-year-old Megan about to chomp down on a garden-variety snail. She burst into tears when I screamed, "Stop!" I ran over to her, grabbed the snail and flung it over the back fence into the canyon.

"But Mommy! *Daddy* likes snails, remember?"

I had to do some fast talking, and needless to say, I was more careful about the sections of Daddy's letters that I read in the future.

It wasn't until my husband left the navy after twenty-six years to begin a civilian career that I made an important discovery about those letters. Who would have thought that, in spite of our countless military separations over twenty-six years in the navy, the letters we exchanged would do more to foster intimacy than if my husband had been at home? I certainly wouldn't have. I'd always been afraid we would grow apart because of Fred's long absences from home. I realized that just the opposite had happened.

One day, when I was "cleaning out," I came upon one of many shoe boxes filled with his letters. Mind you, I'm a firm believer in getting rid of extra "stuff." All those years of moving and "cleaning out" have kept our home organized.

With my hand on the trash can, I asked myself, *Should I toss them out?* Instant heart-pounding panic stopped me. How could I even think such a thing? Fred's letters are valuable pieces of family history. They represented a huge chunk of our lives.

But even more important than that is a profound "aha" that washed over me. My husband and I had felt called to a life of military service, and we had been obedient to that difficult calling through all its joys and hardships. God showed me that our letters were his provision for an intimate relationship, in spite of our many separations.

How could that be, you might ask? As I reflected on

how God had provided intimacy, I saw that my husband had shared deep parts of himself on those precious pieces of paper. Often, he would write to me after a "mid watch," in the early morning hours. All would be quiet onboard ship, and he would describe the sea at night, the serenity of it, the glassy water with a golden moon watching over it. Or he would write about the turbulence of a typhoon and its twelve-foot seas, about a new understanding of God's majesty. How tiny he felt in their mighty, little navy warship. How much he loved me, Kim and Megan.

Those letters are tender, warm and cherished. They are a vital link to the man I love. Even now, it is sometimes difficult to get Fred to expose the vulnerabilities he shared in his mid-watch letters. I doubt we would be as close today if it hadn't been for years of writing to each other, but there's no way of proving that. What makes me feel grateful and amazed is that, in spite of the hardships of military life, God blessed me with one of my deepest desires—a desire I thought impossible because we were apart.

Only God could lay the groundwork for tenderness and intimacy between my husband and me when we were physically separated. And he did that through letters.

Martha Pope Gorris

Grandma's Wisdom

The only thing you can change in the world is yourself, and that makes all the difference in the world.

Cher

I was dreading the six-month deployment. I was going to have to take care of our three-and-a-half-month-old son by myself, was going to be without my best friend for six whole months, and, because we were fairly new in the squadron, I hadn't been able to make friends yet. I could not fathom it.

People gave me a lot of advice, and all of it turned out to be true. One girl said that the anticipation of the separation is much worse than it actually is. Another girl told me that it was the best thing—but she's glad she'll never have to do it again. But all the advice is in one ear and out the other the night before your spouse really leaves.

It was the day of my birthday, and my stomach was in knots. I just wanted him to leave so that we could work on his coming home. I wondered how I was going to get through this.

A few days after he left, I got a piece of advice that really stayed with me. I was on the phone with my eighty-year-old grandmother. She has always given me the best advice, and, especially now, I valued her wisdom.

Grandma Louise said, "You just can't feel sorry for yourself!"

During World War II, Grandpa was gone; he even missed the birth of my mother. So, I knew Grandma knew what she was talking about. As soon as she said those words to me, I could feel my attitude changing. She had handed me her secret.

From that moment on, I never considered it a dreadful thing that my husband was gone. I never considered the separation as a loss. Sure, I missed him, and, yes, I ran to the phone every time it rang. But my pity-party had been officially canceled.

I used my six-month separation wisely. I cherished the 'round-the-clock fun I got to spend with my son. I went on daily walks with him and the dog, and I got to know more of the neighbors. I painted every room in the house. I sewed curtains and pillows. I landscaped the backyard. I grilled burgers and shish kebobs on the barbecue. I mowed the yard and took the trash out every week. I managed the bills and the checkbook. I did things that I had never done before because I couldn't, didn't want to or didn't know how.

Grandma was right, and, by not feeling sorry for myself, I had a lot of time on my hands. Her words of wisdom had changed my entire outlook. It was a gift from one navy wife to another, from a grandma to her granddaughter. She gave me words that I will hear forever, whenever they're needed to be heard.

Rachel E. Twenter

A Trip to Washington, D.C.

*You must learn to be still in the midst of activity
and to be vibrantly alive in repose.*

Indira Gandhi

I wanted to write something special for the June FRG newsletter since the army was celebrating 225 years of service, but I couldn't find the words. I tried writing about Sergeant York and General Bradley, but it all just felt cold. Nothing I wrote conveyed what I had in my mind.

Ultimately, I found my muse in Washington, D.C., while we were sitting in ringside seats, watching the Spirit of America. I was armed with three different cameras that day, and, between the three of them, I must have taken more than a hundred photographs.

I am what my husband calls "a shutterbug." Unless I'm only planning on going to the grocery store, when I leave the house, I bring a camera. Since I started taking pictures, I have longed to catch the perfect moment on film, and, until now, my favorite subjects were my family.

We were sitting so close that I could see the froth on the horses as they fought the bits in their mouths during the cavalry unit show. I thrilled at the pageantry of the army while we watched the drill team and musical corps. And there it was: my dream picture, the photograph of a lifetime, appeared before me.

A retired general from the airborne division—a man in his seventies who had fought in World War II, Korea and Vietnam—sat beside us with his wife. When the 82nd Airborne chorus sang their song, the general stood at attention.

The composition was perfect. I was looking at the back of a soldier who had served his time. He stood as straight as his body would allow. I took in the gray hair, the liver spots on his shaky hands and the stoop in his shoulders. To his right, I saw the chorus, young soldiers with muscular arms and slim waists. The ramrod-straight spines of youth. To his left, I saw his wife's profile. She had been by his side throughout his military career, and was with him today. The love and pride on her face shone clearly in her expression.

In the time it took the chorus to sing the song, I found and lost my perfect photograph. Even though I had those three cameras and plenty of film left, I didn't take it. I didn't want to disturb the sanctity of that moment. But I will keep that image in my mind to remember two things: at heart, a soldier never leaves the army, and a military spouse's pride and love know no timeline.

Abigail L. Hammond

Standing Tall

Anyone who fights for the future lives in it today.

Ayn Rand

Forty-seven cadets have been commissioned today; forty-seven young men and women are prepared to start new careers as lieutenants in the U.S. Army. One officer will retire.

Friends and family have come from all parts of the world to witness the commissioning and my husband's retirement. O'ma has come from Florida, his sister from Texas and his brother from New York. Our daughter is newly home from college, and our son has surprised us both by flying in from Italy. Friends we haven't seen in years are here to share in another big step in our lives.

Looking out on the long room of people drinking wine and eating hors d'oeuvres, my mind wanders back twenty-three years. . . .

Indiantown Gap Military Reservation. The auditorium is packed with friends and family all prepared to watch the event about to take place onstage. Straining to see my husband of a year, I see the colors being presented and the commissionees march onstage. There he is! He stands tall in his newly purchased uniform; the fit is flawless; the creases are perfect. Everything about his appearance shows pride, from the high gloss of his black shoes to the shine of his new brass. He looks young and sure of himself.

The cadets and audience are told to be seated, and Pennsylvania's Senator Carlisle is introduced as guest speaker. His long-winded speech of duty, honor and country seems endless as the audience awaits the swearing in. Finally, General Jeffrey is standing before the cadets asking them to "Stand and repeat after me: I, state your name, do solemnly swear that I will support and defend the Constitution of the United States against all enemies, foreign and domestic; that I will bear true faith and allegiance to the same; and that I will faithfully discharge the duties of the office upon which I am about to enter—so help me God."

It's over. He's a lieutenant. He's a commissioned officer.

"Mom, Mom, we need more fresh fruit for the buffet table. Can you help me?" How like my daughter to drag me from my dreams and force my attention to the immediate.

"Of course, Meg," I respond, as I try to get back to the duties at hand. But this seems to be a day to digress.

How many times have I replenished trays on a buffet table? Has it really been twenty-three years? Twenty-three years of packing household goods and moving around the world to find exciting adventures, good friends and new challenges have gone by so quickly. Where has the time gone?

It seems only yesterday we packed our meager four hundred pounds of belongings and flew to Germany for his first assignment. What great experiences we had exploring the old castles of Wurtzberg and looking for small country *winestubes* so we could sample the local vintage. What long hours he kept at his new job. And then there were the separations. There was the year he spent in Vietnam and his year in Korea. How he missed the kids. We couldn't write enough letters or send enough pictures.

The adventures have been extensive. We lived in old dragoon barracks in Kansas; in quarters built during the Japanese occupation of Korea; on the warm sandy beaches of Florida where our daughter learned how to swim; and in New Mexico, where our son used a waxed Formica ski on the white sand dunes. To think we used to worry about the children and how our nomadic lifestyle would affect their growing up! They have thrived with each of our moves.

The time has gone. . . .

"Mrs. Buchwald, it's time to start. Would you please take your place?"

"Of course, Major Stewart." I am pulled back into the present.

There he is in his uniform for the last time. He stands tall. He's gained a little weight, but not much. His uniform fits well; the creases are perfect. His shoes have a high gloss, and the brass of the uniform is worn but polished. Above his left pocket are the medals that show his commitment to duty, honor and country. He has a touch of gray at his temples and moist eyes as he stares at a distant point at the far end of the room.

"Attention to orders!" says Colonel Jackson. "Buchwald, Clarence R., Jr., Lieutenant Colonel, United States Army Cadet Command, Cornell University, you are retired from active service, released from assignment and duty, and, on July 31, 1989, placed on the retired list. The people of the United States express their thanks and gratitude for your faithful service. Your contributions to the defense of the United States of America are greatly appreciated."

We've made it. All we can do is hug one another while thoughts of twenty-three years tumble through our minds.

Margaret Buchwald

More Chicken Soup?

Many of the stories and poems you have read in this book were submitted by readers like you who had read earlier *Chicken Soup for the Soul* books. We publish at least five or six *Chicken Soup for the Soul* books every year. We invite you to contribute a story to one of these future volumes.

Stories may be up to twelve hundred words, and must uplift or inspire. You may submit an original piece, something you have read or your favorite quotation on your refrigerator door.

To obtain a copy of our submission guidelines and a listing of upcoming *Chicken Soup* books, please write, fax or check our Web site.

Please send your submissions to:

Chicken Soup for the Soul
P.O. Box 30880, Santa Barbara, CA 93130
fax: 805-563-2945
Web site: *www.chickensoup.com*

We will be sure that both you and the author are credited for your submission.

For information about speaking engagements, other books, audiotapes, workshops and training programs, please contact any of our authors directly.

Supporting Others

In the spirit of supporting others, a portion of the proceeds from *Chicken Soup for the Military Wife's Soul* will support Gold Star Wives of America, Inc.

Gold Star Wives of America, Inc., is a nonprofit national service organization. They are dedicated to assisting the widows of servicemen who have given their lives unselfishly, so that we may retain the freedom we all experience today.

For more information or to make a donation to Gold Star Wives, contact:

Gold Star Wives of America, Inc.
P.O. Box 361986
Birmingham, Alabama 35236
888-751-6350
GoldStarWives.org

9318 Bristleone Dr.
Montgomery, Alabama 36117–8826
334-277-0395

Who Is Jack Canfield?

Jack Canfield is one of America's leading experts in the development of human potential and personal effectiveness. He is both a dynamic, entertaining speaker and a highly sought-after trainer. Jack has a wonderful ability to inform and inspire audiences toward increased levels of self-esteem and peak performance.

Jack most recently released a book for success entitled, *The Success Principles: How to Get from Where You Are to Where You Want to Be*. He is the author and narrator of several bestselling audio- and videocassette programs, including *Self-Esteem and Peak Performance, How to Build High Self-Esteem, Self-Esteem in the Classroom* and *Chicken Soup for the Soul—Live*. He is regularly seen on television shows such as *Good Morning America, The Today Show, 20/20* and *Fox and Friends*. Jack has co-authored numerous books, including the *Chicken Soup for the Soul* series, *Dare to Win* and *The Aladdin Factor* (all with Mark Victor Hansen), *100 Ways to Build Self-Concept in the Classroom* (with Harold C. Wells), *Heart at Work* (with Jacqueline Miller) and *The Power of Focus* (with Les Hewitt and Mark Victor Hansen).

Jack is a regularly featured speaker for professional associations, school districts, government agencies, churches, hospitals, sales organizations and corporations. His clients have included the American Dental Association, the American Management Association, AT&T, Campbell's Soup, Clairol, Domino's Pizza, GE, Hartford Insurance, ITT, Johnson & Johnson, the Million Dollar Roundtable, NCR, New England Telephone, Re/Max, Scott Paper, TRW and Virgin Records. Jack has taught on the faculty of Income Builders International, a school for entrepreneurs.

Jack conducts an annual seven-day training called "Breakthrough to Success." It attracts entrepreneurs, educators, counselors, parenting trainers, corporate trainers, professional speakers, ministers and others interested in improving their lives and the lives of others.

For free gifts from Jack and information on his materials and availability, go to:

Web site: *www.jackcanfield.com*
Self-Esteem Seminars
P.O. Box 30880
Santa Barbara, CA 93130
phone: 805-563-2935 • fax: 805-563-2945

Who Is Mark Victor Hansen?

In the area of human potential, no one is more respected than Mark Victor Hansen. For more than thirty years, Mark has focused solely on helping people from all walks of life reshape their personal vision of what's possible. His powerful messages of possibility, opportunity and action have created powerful change in thousands of organizations and millions of individuals worldwide.

He is a sought-after keynote speaker, bestselling author and marketing maven. Mark's credentials include a lifetime of entrepreneurial success and an extensive academic background. He is a prolific writer with many bestselling books such as *The One Minute Millionaire, The Power of Focus, The Aladdin Factor* and *Dare to Win,* in addition to the *Chicken Soup for the Soul* series. Mark has made a profound influence through his library of audios, videos and articles in the areas of big thinking, sales achievement, wealth building, publishing success, and personal and professional development.

Mark is the founder of the MEGA Seminar Series. MEGA Book Marketing University and Building Your MEGA Speaking Empire are annual conferences where Mark coaches and teaches new and aspiring authors, speakers and experts on building lucrative publishing and speaking careers. Other MEGA events include MEGA Marketing Magic and My MEGA Life.

He has appeared on television (*Oprah,* CNN and *The Today Show*), in print (*Time, U.S. News & World Report, USA Today, New York Times* and *Entrepreneur*) and on countless radio interviews, assuring our planet's people that "You can easily create the life you deserve."

As a philanthropist and humanitarian, Mark works tirelessly for organizations such as Habitat for Humanity, American Red Cross, March of Dimes, Childhelp USA and many others. He is the recipient of numerous awards that honor his entrepreneurial spirit, philanthropic heart and business acumen. He is a lifetime member of the Horatio Alger Association of Distinguished Americans, an organization that honored Mark with the prestigious Horatio Alger Award for his extraordinary life achievements.

Mark Victor Hansen is an enthusiastic crusader of what's possible and is driven to make the world a better place.

Mark Victor Hansen & Associates, Inc.
P.O. Box 7665
Newport Beach, CA 92658
phone: 949-764-2640
fax: 949-722-6912
Visit Mark online at: *www.markvictorhansen.com*

Who Is Cindy Pedersen?

Cindy is currently the publisher of *KITPLANES* magazine, a title sold worldwide to individuals who build and fly their own private aircraft. She has spent the past twenty-eight years in broadcasting and publishing. In addition to the current Chicken Soup project, she cofounded the charitable foundation (not-for-profit) Web site: *www.militarysoul.org* with coauthor and business associate, Charles Preston. The interactive portal is designed to make a positive difference in the lives of military troops, their families and patriots.

Cindy was raised in western New York and now makes Southern California her home. She comes from an entrepreneurial family with a long history of military service. Her grandfather served in World War I, father in World War II, husband in the Bay of Pigs, and her son is currently in the Army Reserve. She is the proud mother of Tina and Anthony, and "Granny" to Brandon.

When not working, Cindy enjoys the beach, jazz, theater, world travel, and church and community activities.

She can be reached at:

MilitarySoul.org
P.O. Box 1501
Solana Beach, CA 92075
phone: 760-942-5483
e-mail: *cindy@militarysoul.org*
Web site: *www.militarysoul.org*

Who Is Charles Preston?

Charles Preston is the senior advertising manager for *KITPLANES* magazine, a title sold worldwide to individuals who build and fly their own private aircraft. In addition to coauthoring *Chicken Soup for the Military Wife's Soul*, he cofounded the charitable foundation (not-for-profit) Web site: *www.militarysoul.org* with coauthor and business associate, Cindy Pedersen. The interactive portal is designed to make a positive difference in the lives of military troops, their families and patriots. He has more than thirty years of experience in marketing and advertising.

Charles followed a family tradition of military service by joining the U.S. Navy in 1966. He served aboard the USS *Arlington* AGMR–2 and as a yeoman on the staff of Commander Cruiser-Destroyer Group 3. He served two tours of duty in Vietnam.

Charles is an avid antique shopper, car buff and photographer. His other interests include flying, ice hockey, gardening and spending time on the beach.

Charles was born and raised in St. Paul, Minnesota. He currently resides in Southern California with his wife Robin. Together, they are active in local concerns.

He can be reached at:

Militarysoul.org
P.O. Box 1501
Solana Beach, CA 92075
phone: 760-942-5483
e-mail: *charles@militarysoul.org*
Web site: *www.militarysoul.org*

Contributors

The majority of stories in this book were submitted by military spouses, veterans and family members of the armed forces in response to our call-out for stories. If you would like to contact any of the contributors for information about their writing or would like to invite them to speak in your community, look for their contact information included in their biographies.

Julie Angelo received her bachelor's degree in education from Youngstown State. She has been a military spouse for more than sixteen years and has taught in Texas and Louisiana. Currently living in Ohio, she is doing the toughest job of all—raising children! She can be reached at *j4angelo@ earthlink.net*.

Both **Megan Armstrong** and her husband serve their country from Washington State: He is in the army, and she is in the air force. They were married in 2003, and because of a related article, had a picture and story of their wedding featured on the front page of the *Seattle Post Intelligencer* on Saturday, March 1, 2003.

Steven Arrington (Col., USAF—Ret.) is a decorated combat veteran and retired after thirty years of service. He's been married to Jane for twenty-eight years, and his tribute to all military spouses was born from his observations—and quiet admiration—of the numerous sacrifices he watched her make through eighteen PCS moves.

Tracy Atkins received a bachelor's degree in business from the University of Maryland in 1998. She and her husband, MJ, have two children, Brittany and Michael Jr. She enjoys traveling, reading and volunteering.

Patricia Barbee grew up and was educated in Boston. She began writing in the fifth grade. She has written for various publications and is a published fiction author. She met her late marine husband in church in Boston the same week he arrived on the USS *Wasp*.

Susanna Hickman Bartee received degrees in history and journalism from Southern Methodist University in 1990. She and her husband have four children. In 2004, she launched *www.militarymama.net*, a unique and humorous look at the military lifestyle. She can be reached at *contact_us@militarymama.net*.

Melissa Baumann is a freelance writer (wishing for a job), navy wife and mother of three boys whose antics practically deliver column fodder. She's also a full-time college student, Webmaster and fund-raising guru for her sons' crew team in Chesapeake, Virginia. She can be reached at *melissabaumann@cox.net*.

Jessica Blankenbecler is fourteen years old and a sophomore in high school. She loves the sun and swimming, and enjoys writing in her journal. She plans to go on to college, but her field of study is unknown at this time.

William H. Blankfield Jr. (Col., USAF—Ret.) received a B.A. from Lasalle College (now University) in Philadelphia in 1949. He taught school (history, geography and Latin) until being recalled to active duty in 1951. He was commissioned in 1952 and spent most of his twenty-six years in the service in communications/electronics. His service included two years during World War II. He retired in 1974 and has been basking in idleness ever since—busy idleness, of course.

Carrie Boggs currently resides on a farm with her husband, Jeremy, in the beautiful hills of Tennessee. The couple is very active at Gum Springs Baptist Church near their home. The couple enjoys the outdoors and spending time with their families. She can be reached at *carrieboggs@hotmail.com*.

Heidi Boortz received her B. A. in English/creative writing from the University of Wisconsin–Eau Claire in 1996. She has two young sons, and they are her inspiration for children's stories she would like to publish someday.

Margaret Buchwald was the quintessential "camp follower" for twenty-three years. She mastered the art of wives' clubs, raising children and pets, managing husband and soldier, and years of separation. After receiving her bachelor's and master's degrees later in life, she is now an English teacher in Palm Beach, Florida.

Saundra L. Butts is a youth pastor, navy wife and mother of three residing in Virginia Beach, Virginia. She received bachelor of arts degrees in American government and rhetoric and communication studies from the University of Virginia in 1983. She is currently working on her master's degree in Christian ministry at Asbury Theological Seminary, and enjoys writing, reading, softball and golf. She can be reached at *saunnieb@yahoo.com*.

Candace Carteen has obtained several degrees. She's a Toastmaster (CTM-B), mother of one son and wife to her beloved best friend. Candace enjoys swimming, reading, skating and playing with her family. She's currently seeking a publisher for a book series she's written. She can be reached at *scribe@ aemail4u.com*. (Note: Yes, she owns the picture.)

Mary Catherine Carwile has just published her first book, *Heartstrings at 35,000 Feet*. Her contribution is from that book. Her book holds a collection of personal stories she garnered in her job as a flight attendant: from conversations she had with passengers—stories about tragedy, happiness, romance, family, courage, friendship and heroism. Mary can be reached at *www.marycarwile.com*.

Mary C. Chace is a seasoned army wife, who has navigated combat deployments, cross-country moves and long separations from her favorite helicopter pilot, all while homeschooling their large family. She is currently developing a freelance career from their home near Fort Campbell, Kentucky. She can be reached at *mary.chace@us.army.mil*.

Roxanne Chase is a U.S. Air Force veteran. Her poem was inspired by her "flyboy" husband Sergeant Reed Chase. Roxanne enjoys writing, cooking and entertaining. Her biggest joy, however, comes from raising her daughter Hayven. She can be reached at *r-rchase@sbcglobal.net.*

Amie Clark is currently a home daycare provider for military families. She attended Ashland University in Ohio and is currently working on her elementary-education degree. Amie is a wife and mother of two boys. In her free time, she enjoys swimming, reading and spending time with her family. She would like to take up painting when her children are a little older. She can be reached at *clarkfamily24@netzero.net.*

Lisa Cobb is a registered nurse and an army wife. She is the mother of three children. She and her family have traveled extensively during their seventeen years of service. She enjoys caring for her family and outdoor activities. Professionally, she enjoys hospice work and teaching childbirth classes.

Dianne Collier, author, columnist and military wife for more than thirty-five years, has experienced firsthand the unique challenges faced by military families. In her bestselling book, *My Love, My Life* (2004), Dianne turns to military spouses from across Canada, the United States, and overseas to tell their stories. She can be reached at *info@mylovemylife.ca.*

Jill Cottrell is an army wife of eight and a half years. She has been active in the army community, receiving numerous awards for her volunteer work, for bettering the lives of soldiers and their families. She currently resides at Fort Benning, Georgia, with her husband Paul, their eight-year-old twin daughters and four-year-old son.

Joanne Danna has been a secretary for the New Jersey Department of Military and Veterans Affairs in Cumberland County. Over the years, as a widow of a Vietnam veteran, she has had several experiences with the Gold Star Wives of America. She enjoys painting, the beach and spending time with her two grandchildren.

Jude Dennis lives with her second husband on a 1939 wooden boat in Oregon. Together, they own and run a company committed to designing and manufacturing products that help more military personnel return home safely. Her sister, Mary Kramer, a professional writer, helped her compose what was in her heart.

Mary E. Dess received her master's degree in English from Sacramento State University and taught English at American River College in Sacramento. She has written for *The Retired Officer's* magazine, *Young Miss, Home Life, Woman's World, The Woman* and various Christian publications. Mary, her husband and five children traveled extensively as a military family.

After twenty-five years as an air force wife, **Twink DeWitt**—with her husband, Denny—serves with Mercy Ships and Youth with a Mission. She enjoys helping others write family stories that become legacies for future generations. The

DeWitts have three married sons and five grandchildren. She can be reached at *dewitt@tyler.net*.

Theresa Doss received her bachelor of arts from Mount Marty College in Yankton, South Dakota, in 1995. She currently teaches at the middle-school level, and also speaks to young audiences about self-esteem issues and mother/daughter relationships. She can be reached at *imadoss@hotmail.com*.

Amy J. Fetzer is the daughter, wife and mother of career U.S. Marines. A best-selling author, she aptly marked her thirtieth published novel with *Tell It to the Marines* (action-adventure, Brava, December 2004). After twenty-five years of traveling with the Corps, Amy and her family live outside Charleston, South Carolina, enjoying the quiet, retired life and trying to behave like civilians. Visit her Web site: *www.amyjfetzer.com*.

Diane L. Flowers is married and the mother of one young son and two stepchildren. Her husband was called to active duty in February 2003, and was sent to the Middle East for Operation Enduring Freedom, where he remained until December 2003. Diane lives with her husband and son in Maryland.

When **Jane Garvey's** husband retired from the military, their family settled in small-town Westerville, Ohio. Jane loves batik, watercolor, oil and silk painting, and writing. If asked for a favorite pastime, she will say she hasn't decided what to be when she grows up. She can be reached at *tagfree@sbcglobal.net*.

Martha Pope Gorris received her bachelor of arts in English/creative writing from George Mason University while her husband, a career naval officer, was assigned to duty at the Pentagon. Her first book, *Held Captive by Futile Thoughts? Break Free!* was published in 2000.

Sally B. Griffis is a licensed professional counselor in private practice in Peachtree City, Georgia. Sally is a frequent speaker, TV guest and presenter for numerous organizations across the country. Her current project is a book, *On the Back of the Beast,* featuring the stories of courageous military survivors. She can be reached at *Sallyg54@aol.com*.

Sue Groseclose-Combs was born and raised in Dayton, Ohio. She graduated from Wright State University with a sociology degree. She married her husband Bill in 1978, becoming a military wife the same year. Sue has taught preschool and served in numerous volunteer positions. She can be reached at *billandsue@mindspring.com*.

Gail Gross is a Christian author and counselor currently working as director of Westbrook Health Services in Spencer, West Virginia. Her husband retired from the U.S. Army in September 2004, and they moved from Germany back to the States, residing now in Ripley, West Virginia. She can be reached at *gail@kinggross.com*.

Nancy Hall is a navy spouse with prior navy military service. She was a volunteer ombudsman (liaison between military families and Seabee Battalion

Commanding Officer) during Desert Storm. The Halls have recently retired, live in an RV full-time and are traveling throughout the United States to discover its history.

Abigail L. Hammond has been an army wife for thirteen years and is the mother of four children. She enjoys cross-stitching, photography and reading. She is active in her Family Readiness Group and Army Family Team Building, and has won numerous awards for her volunteer efforts. She can be reached at *abigail.hammond@us.army.mil.*

Jonny Hawkins is a nationally known cartoonist from Sherwood, Michigan. Thousands of his cartoons have been published in magazines such as *Reader's Digest, Guidepost's, Saturday Evening Post, Harvard Business Review, Boy's Life* and over 250 others. He lives with his wife, Carissa and their two young sons, Nathaniel and Zachary. He can be reached at 616-432-8071 or at P.O. Box 188 Sherwood, MI 49089, or via e-mail at *cartoonist@anthill.com.*

Amy Hollingsworth is a military wife to U.S. Marine Sergeant James Hollingsworth and a stay-at-home mother to Abigail and Jacob. They currently are stationed in beautiful Hawaii and look forward to living the military life for many more years to come.

Jan Hornung, military mate (army wife) and former army helicopter pilot, is the author of five books, including *This Is the Truth as Far as I Know: I Could Be Wrong* (humorous stories of married to military and life) and *Angels in Vietnam: Women Who Served.* Her Web site is *www.geocities.com/vietnamfront.*

Carol Howard is currently working on her associate's degree. She enjoys writing and is an avid reader. She has three wonderful children and is happily married to her own personal hero. Carol is writing a historical romance novel and hopes to one day see it published. She can be reached at *williamandcarol howard@yahoo.com.*

Denise J. Hunnell has been a military spouse for twenty years. She is also the mother of four children and a family-practice physician. Home is where the air force sends her family. Denise writes about family issues from her current home in northern Virginia. She can be reached at *hunnell.family@cox.net.*

Terry Hurley is a retired U.S. Army major. She lives in Woodbridge, Virginia, with her husband, an active-duty officer, and their young son. Terry enjoys volunteer work and home-improvement projects. She plans to write her autobiography some day. She can be reached at *bhurley27@aol.com.*

Mary D. Jackson was born in March 1923, to Adelia and Charles Drummer in Ottawa, Ohio, the seventh of ten children. She married Barton Campbell, who was serving our country as a Naval Chief Petty Officer. She had five brothers who served in the war, all of whom returned home safely. Barton did not return from action in the Pacific to see their son Michael grow up. Upon retirement from the New York City childcare system, she began to write her life story, *Some Are Magic and Some Are Tragic.*

Michael J. Jett graduated from Wake Forest University and the University of North Carolina at Chapel Hill. His first novel, *Secret Games,* was published in 2003. A financial executive, he resides in Phoenix and is working on his second novel. He can be reached at *mjcrj@cox.net.*

Angela Keane is the proud military wife to Lt. Dan Keane, U.S. Coast Guard. She is a stay-at-home mom to their two children, Braeden and Morgan. Angela enjoys traveling, shopping, reading, scrapbooking and spending time with her family. She can be reached at *coastiefamily@sbcglobal.net.*

Jilleen Kesler is currently a housewife living in Southern California. Between the navy moving her around frequently, raising her children and proudly supporting her husband through his naval career, she is working on her first of hopefully many novels. She can be reached at *skjk01@yahoo.com.*

Born in Buna, Texas, **Stacy Smith Kirchheiner** has been writing poetry that reflects her love of God and family. She has been married for sixteen years to Richard. They have four children and enjoy the navy life of travel. She can be reached at *living4heaven2002@yahoo.com.*

Kelli Kirwan is the wife of a U.S. Marine and a mother of six. She's written for *GoodSense* magazine and a weekly column in the *El Paso Times.* Kelli plans to write a book on raising children in the military and speaks about families and military life. She can be reached at *wadeentp@sbcglobal.net.*

Debbie Koharik is an air force wife who served on active duty for nine years. She has an M.A. in English and has taught ESL and English composition courses. Currently, she is a full-time, work-at-home mother of two and a part-time writer of children's stories. She can be reached at *dkoharik@earthlink.net.*

Krystee Kott received her bachelor of science in ocean engineering from the United States Naval Academy in 1995. She enjoys traveling, running, reading and hiking with her husband. Krystee is currently cowriting a young-adult novel with her father, Michael Kott. She can be reached at *krysteek@hotmail.com.*

Amanda Legg is a proud wife, mother and daughter. She is in the process of going back to college for her nursing degree at Central Texas College. Amanda enjoys spending time with her family, watching old movies and camping.

Tammy C. Logan is a military wife of eight years and has at least twelve more years to go. She relocated to three different duty stations with her husband Jim. In addition, she has supported and held her family together through three deployments. They have one son who is the light of their life. Tammy is currently a third-grade teacher with the Department of Defense Education System, at Fort Benning. Her passions include teaching and spending quality time with her family.

Gary Luerding, a retired army NCO, has been married to Lynne for forty-two years and has three children and eight grandchildren. He enjoys fishing, pyrography and writing. Published works include *Inshore Ocean Fishing for*

Dummies (San-Dal' Publications ©1994), and "Beyond the Breakers" (*Chicken Soup for the Fisherman's Soul*).

Elizabeth Martin, a registered nurse, is the wife of a career military officer, mother of two grown children and grandmother of three young grandsons. Her father was a World War II veteran who was wounded on Iwo Jima. Her brother, son-in-law and son are also military veterans.

Shelley Lynn McEwan lives in Sarna, Ontario, with her husband Gord and their sons Joshua, Adam and Noah. She is an early childhood educator in the Ontario Early Years Program at Labton College. "Letter of Hope" was written for Gord's grandparents, William and Martha Lindsay, who are now together in heaven, never again to be parted.

Shelly Mecum is an inspirational speaker and the author of the award-winning book *God's Photo Album*. Her work has been featured on Dr. Robert Schuller's *Hour of Power*, PAX TV's *It's a Miracle*, *Guideposts Magazine* and *Chicken Soup from the Soul of Hawaii*. The University of San Diego presented her with the prestigious 2001 Author E. Hughes Career Achievement Award. This former navy ombudsman and proud wife of a retired navy chief is currently at work on other writing projects. She can be reached at *www.godsphotoalbum.com*.

Jennifer Minor received her bachelor of arts degree in French from Valparaiso University in 1997. She married Kevin, now a captain in the air force in 1998. She stays at home with their two young daughters, Hannah and Hope. She enjoys traveling, writing, playing sports and spending time with her family.

Sarah Clark Monagle is a guidance counselor, currently a stay-at-home mom to three daughters. She is also the proud wife of a navy helicopter pilot. She earned a B.A. in sociology in 1990 and an M.Ed. in counseling in 1992. She can be reached at *sarahmonagle@yahoo.com*.

Amy Naegeli, twenty-eight, is a military wife to her best friend and husband of six years. She is currently earning a degree in elementary education. When Amy is not chasing after her two-year-old son, she enjoys cooking, movies, books and crafts. She can be reached at *amynaegeli75@hotmail.com*.

Ann Hail Norris holds a bachelor of science degree from Southwestern College. She owns Norris Consulting and Design, a professional writing and layout business, in Sheerwood, Arkansas. Between work and raising her military family, Ann volunteers her time and talents to various nonprofit organizations. She can be reached at *annie722@aol.com*.

Kathy Oberhaus, a former flight attendant for a major airline, met her husband during his internship for Special Operations' most sophisticated helicopter, the MH-53 Pave Low. To unite spouses, she created numerous productions to entertain and promote morale of active-duty military. She and her husband are the proud parents of three children. Currently, she is pursuing legislative changes to protect the elderly.

Jennifer Anne Oscar is a 1997 graduate of Embry-Riddle Aeronautical University and former army intelligence officer. She and her active-duty husband have four children. Her passions include family, quilting, scrapbooking and skiing back in Colorado. She also volunteers helping other military spouses. She can be reached at *scoilb@hotmail.com*.

After graduating from Sophia University, Tokyo, **Marilyn Pate** taught both children and adults. In addition to family and writing, her interests include researching pioneer women's stories, Western history and stitchery. She and her retired navy husband, married for more than fifty years, live near Tucson, Arizona.

Thomas D. Phillips (Colonel, USAF—Ret.) led a detachment through a Red Brigades terrorist episode, served as director of the Air Force Personnel Readiness Center during Operation Desert Storm and commanded troops in Bosnia. He and his wife Nita, a registered nurse, reside in Lincoln, Nebraska.

MSgt. Benjamin Pigsley will retire from active duty in the U.S. Army in May 2005 with more than twenty-one years of dedicated service. He and his wife Julie have been married for seventeen years, and have two children, Daniel Joseph, age sixteen, and Samantha Nichole, age fourteen.

Donna Porter is a freelance writer, mother and proud air force spouse. Her husband, SSgt. Douglas Porter, and their three children, Carrington, Jensen and Emmalyn, are currently stationed at Landstuhl Teginal Medical Center in Germany. Donna enjoys crocheting, reading and spending time with the family. She can be reached at *buggaboosmommy@yahoo.com*.

Diane Proulx holds a B.A. in history and M.Ed. in curriculum and instructions. She retired from Verizon and currently teaches U.S. history and civics in New Hampshire. Diane and her husband have two sons. She enjoys traveling and reading. She can be reached at *dlproulx.@comcast.net*.

Michele Putman is a twice-published poet, but her true passion lies in suspense thrillers. She works for a successful restaurant chain in Arizona where she is continuing her education. Michele spends her free moments scrapbooking, gardening, hiking and spending time with her two daughters and partner in crime, James. Michele is currently writing another nonfiction book and hopes to have it published within the next few years.

Elizabeth Rae is a wife and mother. She has an associate's degree. She enjoys gardening and walking and has a strong faith in God. She was raised in a military family, and has two sons and a husband who served in Operation Iraqi Freedom. She is proud to be an American.

Sonja R. Ragaller currently lives in Virginia and has been married for twenty-one years to Rick. Together, they have two beautiful children, Nicolas and Sabrina. Sonja is very proud to be both the wife and the daughter of military servicemen, and would like to thank all who serve and sacrifice for our country.

Kim Riley is an army wife of more than thirteen years. She and her husband George are New Jersey natives who currently live near Fort Campbell, Kentucky, with their boys Josh, twelve, and Kevin, eight. Kim enjoys spending time with her family as well as substitute teaching and volunteering at her boys' schools.

Gwen C. Rollings received her bachelor of arts degree, magna cum laude, and is a master of human communication. She has written a book of poetry, *Seasons of a Woman*, owns a training and development business, and conducts Christian women's seminars. Married since 1966 to Maj. Gen. Wayne Rollings (USMC—Ret.), they have four children. She can be reached at *rollingstraining@aol.com*.

Sara Rosett received her bachelor of arts from Texas Tech University, graduating summa cum laude. She is a military spouse, stay-at-home mom and writer. Her stories and essays appear in several anthologies. She is the author of the Military Mom Mystery series. She can be reached at *www.sararosett.com*.

Tammy Ross is a three-time cancer survivor and believes that miracles happen every day. She has two children, Kayla and Anna. She gives thanks to God daily for the protection he provided to her husband Terry during his service in Baghdad. She can be reached at *TerryTLRoss@aol.com*.

Kimberly L. Shaffer earned her bachelor of science from Salisbury University in 1993. She teaches fourth grade in a rural elementary school overlooking the Potomac River. Kim and her solider husband Joe have been married for eleven years. They have a nine-year-old son and a four-year-old daughter. She can be reached at *jkak@gcnetmail.net*.

Tracey L. Sherman married her high-school sweetheart, now a twenty-two-year veteran, twenty-five years ago. Prior, Tracey was a lifelong air force brat. The mother of three awesome children, Tracey is certified to teach English and actively pursues her dream of writing for children and young adults. She can be reached at *TraceyLSherman@aol.com*.

Sarah Smiley is the author of "Shore Duty," a weekly syndicated newspaper column for military spouses. In October 2005, New American Library will release her first book, *Going Overboard*. Stay tuned to *www.SarahSmiley.com* for more details.

Alice Faye Smith is the mother of three and grandmother of nine, wife of ex-Seabee Jerry Smith for forty-one years. She taught herself to type and considers her writing ability as a gift from God. Her stories capture her love for her God, her family and her America.

Jodie Cain Smith received her bachelor of fine arts degree from the University of South Alabama in 1999. In 2003, Jodie began the column "Married to the Military." She enjoys theater, crafts and, most of all, time with her husband. She can be reached at: *jodie.cainsmith@us.army.mil*.

Kristin Spurlock is a native of Dover, Ohio, and a graduate of Bowling Green

324 CONTRIBUTORS

State University with a bachelor of fine arts degree. She and her husband Brian have one son, Drew, and are currently stationed at Fort Riley, Kansas, where she volunteers her time to several military-family organizations.

Naomi Stanton received her B.A. from Bradley University in 1995. She is the proud mommy to three children and married to Capt. Paul T. Stanton, the love of her life. She can be reached at *paulstanton6@hotmail.com*.

Joyce Stark lives in northeast Scotland and splits her time between her writing and working for the community mental-health team. She is currently writing a children's series to promote early learning of a second language and a cookbook entitled *You Put WHAT in It?*

Chanda Stelter is a devoted wife and loving mother living in North Dakota, where she enjoys the diversity of seasonal changes. Throughout her husband's deployment she realized that each day is a gift with a purpose. She is a woman who commits every day to glorifying God. She can be reached at *chanda@bis.midco.net*.

Mashawn Sticca received her bachelor of arts degree from Fort Lewis College in 1995. She is currently a stay-at-home mom enjoying volunteering with many different groups in Fort Riley. Mashawn enjoys quilting, walking, reading and working with children. She can be reached at *mashawns@aol.com*.

Sharon C. Stephens Trippe is a retired businesswoman. She was born in Oklahoma, and, being married to a career military man, has lived and traveled most of the world. Sharon's current project is a book for children of divorce, and the love of a horse. She can be reached at *boatswainshar@aol.com*.

Leah Tucker has been married to her soldier since 1993. Together, they have an autistic son who is a joy. With her husband's work, Leah feels it is important to maintain some sort of stability for their son Thomas. They had another child in November 2004, a girl named Rylee. Leah enjoys her job as a technology manager. In her free time, she is a graphic artist and a volunteer for Family Readiness Groups.

Rachel Twenter graduated from the University of Missouri in 1999, where she received a bachelor of arts in communication. She is a wife and mother of two boys. In her free time, she paints children's artwork for her business cREaTe (*www.cREaTebyRET.com*).

Vicki A. Vadala-Cummings grew up on Cape Cod in Massachusetts, and is currently living on Cape Ann, where she teaches elementary school. For thirty-two years she traveled extensively, living and teaching on three continents and in five states in the United States. She has been published in The International Library of Poetry.

Linda Valle is the wife of Air Force Lt. Col. JC Valle and mother of two teenagers, Tara and John. They currently live in Stuttgart, Germany. Linda enjoys antiquing and traveling. Her story is dedicated to the 34th Bomb Squadron families, "The T-Birds."

Lora Vivas, M.Ed, is a literacy specialist and life coach in Colorado, who also teaches yoga, meditation and life skills to children and adults. She considers being the mother of two her most important role. Her children's book will be published in 2005. She can be reached at *loravivas@earthlink.net.*

Bethany Watkins received her B.A. in 1993 from Salve Regina University in Newport, Rhode Island, and her M.S. in educational technology from TSU in 2000. She is the mother of three children and has been a military wife since 1993. Bethany's hobbies include cake decorating, writing, computers, traveling, cooking and reading.

DeEtta Woffinden Anderson is the wife of a military man whose assignments introduced her to many and daily changes of culture, ideas and challenges. At the golden age of eighty-something, this is DeEtta's second published work, her first being in *Chicken Soup for the Fisherman's Soul.* She may be reached at *DeEtta@fishsoul.com.*